Contemporary
Irish Knits

Contemporary Irish Knits

Carol Feller

WILEY

John Wiley & Sons, Inc.

credits

SENIOR EDITOR
Roxane Cerda

PROJECT EDITOR
Carol Pogoni

TECHNICAL EDITOR
Kristi Porter

SENIOR EDITORIAL MANAGER
Christina Stambaugh

VICE PRESIDENT AND PUBLISHER
Cindy Kitchel

VICE PRESIDENT AND EXECUTIVE PUBLISHER
Kathy Nebenhaus

INTERIOR DESIGN
Lissa Auciello-Brogan

ILLUSTRATORS
Ronda David-Burroughs
Cheryl Grubbs

COVER DESIGN
Wendy Mount

PHOTOGRAPHY
Joseph Feller

This book is dedicated with all my love to Caelen, Damien, Dylan, and Lucas.

acknowledgments

This book was a labor of love; I got to knit with wonderful yarns, work with great people, and write about my design philosophy and Ireland. Knitting in Ireland is exploding with activity and I'm delighted that I am able to make my own contribution to it. All of the people I've met while researching this book have inspired me with their enthusiasm for both yarn and knitting.

There are so many people to whom I owe my thanks, in particular:

To the millers and hand dyers who contributed both their yarn and time to make this book possible: Andrew Eadie (Kerry Woollen Mills), Philip Cushen (Cushendale Woollen Mills), Chris Weiniger (Donegal Yarns), Beata Jezekova (Hedgehog Fibres), and Yvonne Kehoe and Elana McSwiney (Dublin Dye Company).

To the many yarn shop owners around Ireland, who were full of encouragement and are eagerly awaiting a book using Irish yarn. A special thanks to This Is Knit; their dedication to home-grown talent helps keep this industry growing in Ireland.

To the professional and dedicated team at Wiley, particularly Roxane Cerda and Carol Pogoni, who patiently answered all my questions and guided this project through the publishing process.

To the models who happily stood in front of the camera: Eleanor Murphy, Amelie Punter, Ted Murphy, Phil Cullen, Caelen Feller, Dylan Feller, Lucas Feller, Clare Murphy, Ciara Murphy, and Claire Murphy.

To my technical editor, Kristi Porter, for catching the errors and for helping me get this book project off the ground in the first place.

To my sample knitter, Sue Cullen, and my test knitters, Emily Snyder and Chris Powell.

To all knitters who have taken classes with me and knitted my patterns, you are my constant encouragement and inspiration.

To my four sons, for enduring many trips around the country to mills, and for tolerating a yarn-obsessed mother who is often knitting when she should be cooking dinner!

Finally, this book would never have come to fruition without the constant encouragement of my wonderful husband, Joseph Feller, who also provided the superb photography in this book.

A very big "thank you" to all of you.

Table of Contents

INTRODUCTION

In my mind, tradition is not like a fossil; it is not some relic of the past. Instead, it's a living thing—a heritage that each new generation takes ownership of, and then nurtures and changes through their own creativity and industry. The collection of patterns in this book are "traditional" in this sense. This book is my attempt to contribute to the rich heritage of knitting in Ireland, and to share this heritage with a wider community of knitters and yarn lovers.

Many different aspects of Irish knitting heritage inspired these patterns. These designs make use of the unmistakable texture of cabled Aran stitches. Aran knitting has long been marketed to the rest of the world as a quintessentially Irish craft. It is surrounded by a romantic mythology of "family patterns" being handed down across generations, similar to how Scottish clans handed down their unique tartan plaids from one generation to the next. However, much of what people know about the history of Aran patterns is half-truth and misconception; it is, in fact, a knitting style created out of necessity during the twentieth century. The earliest recorded appearance of an Aran sweater was from the 1930s and 1940s (a sample is on display at the National Museum in Dublin, Ireland). By the 1950s, women living on the Aran Islands were encouraged to knit on a commercial basis, because there was little other employment on the islands and their knitted sweaters sold well.

The fact that the Aran sweater is not a centuries-old creation does not make it any less important to Ireland's knitting heritage; the innovation and expertise of the Aran women who knit these sweaters should not be undervalued. They took what was a financial necessity and created masterpieces with their knitted work, allowing their personalities and craftsmanship to shine through in their finished products. Inspired by their craft, I combined the intricate interweaving of traditional Aran cables with my own imagination to create the contemporary patterns you will find in this book.

These patterns are also called "Irish" because they are shaped by the unique characteristics of Irish yarn. Ireland has a long history of yarn milling, which was once a very large industry. Due to rising costs and reduced demand, all but a few mills are now

The Aran Islands

The Aran Islands are located off the western coast of Ireland, close to the mouth of Galway Bay. Three islands make up the Aran Islands: Inis Mór (Big Island), Inis Meáin (Middle Island), and Inis Oírr (East Island). Surrounded by the Atlantic Ocean, and frequently cut off from the mainland due to harsh winter weather, the islanders are a self-sufficient people. Their isolated location has meant that both the Irish language and a great deal of traditional Irish heritage has been preserved on these islands. For more information, check out www.aranislands.ie.

closed. While most of the remaining Irish mills primarily produce yarn for weaving cloth, three mills continue to produce yarn for hand knitting on a commercial basis. Their yarns are featured in the first three sections of this book. Yarn from Irish sheep creates coarse but hardwearing and durable wool. Modern Irish mills know that knitting tastes have changed and that many knitters desire a finer grade of yarn. Irish mills have risen to the challenge of merging the traditional with the new by blending softer New Zealand fleeces with Irish fleeces to create a softer Irish blend. This creates a yarn that offers the best of both worlds; it's a little softer, but still hardwearing and durable enough to create a finished product that will stand the test of time. However, the yarns that these mills produce remain distinctly Irish; they are deeply textured, multi-hued yarns that are tweedy and come in a range of lush colors.

For me, a sense of heritage and inspiration comes from the remaining Irish mills. The experience and knowledge that the millers bring to their yarn comes from several generations that have worked with textiles. Specifically, I am impressed by the ways in which they move forward—by listening to the knitting community and by innovating their manufacturing processes—while retaining the treasures of the past (like the distinctive flecks, technically called "nepps," of Donegal tweed).

The final section of this book features patterns that use hand-dyed yarn created by a new generation of Irish yarn producers: the hand dyers. Although the wool they use may come from around the world, they are a key part of Ireland's contemporary, living tradition and the complex, vibrant yarns they create are an inspiration to me as both a designer and a knitter.

Finally, I think of this pattern collection as being part of the Irish knitting tradition because it was inspired by my own Irish heritage and my experiences of growing up and living in Ireland. I learned to knit in

The Origins of Aran Knitting

It is believed that the historian Heinz Kiewe, author of *The Sacred History of Knitting,* is largely responsible for our common (but mostly incorrect) beliefs about Aran knitting traditions. For details about Aran history (and the history of our misconceptions), take a look at:

- "The History of Aran Knitting" (http://www.dochara.com/things-to-buy/aran-knitwear/)
- *The Aran Sweater* (Appletree Press [IE],1993), by Deirdre McQuillan
- *A History of Hand Knitting* (Interweave Press, 2003), by Richard Rutt (reprint)

NOTE: *These books may be difficult to find at bookstores or through online retailers, but you may be able to find them in your local library.*

primary (elementary) school at age six, along with the rest of my class. I have vivid memories of double-pointed needles, lemon acrylic yarn, and fingerless gloves. After that, I knit for several years, producing vests for myself as well as a full wardrobe for my dolls. However, as the years went on I forgot about my knitting, and it wasn't until after the birth of my fourth son that I rediscovered it. When I started knitting again as an adult, I found it to be a rewarding creative outlet with the added benefit of producing functional clothing that looked and felt beautiful. If you can't find a wool cardigan for your baby, well, just knit your own! Although I only rediscovered knitting as an adult, my family has a strong knitting tradition. My grandmother was a wonderful knitter; in fact, every September when my mum went back to school, the nuns would examine her new jumper (sweater) carefully to see what wonder my grandmother had produced that summer. My grandmother took great pride in her knitting, but it was still primarily a functional tool to clothe her family.

My transition from knitter to designer took me quite by surprise. I have an unusual background that combines art and engineering. I attended art college, where I loved to work with textiles but, to my surprise, missed math. After completing a foundation course, I left art school and studied structural engineering at university. While I enjoyed both subjects, neither was, on its own, completely satisfying. After rediscovering knitting, I quickly recognized the similarities it had to engineering. Each stitch is like a little building block and with correct gauge and a bit of imagination (and simple math) there is nothing you can't create with a knitted fabric. This revelation opened the gates for me as a designer and I let my imagination run free, knowing that applying my engineering to my knitting could produce some very innovative results!

The patterns in this book reflect my great loves in knitting: rich colors and complex textures. This book showcases the colors and textures of the Irish landscape, of Irish wools, and of the innovative stitches of Aran knitters. Like my grandmother, I love functional yet durable garments, but the granddaughter in me loves a tailored, flattering fit. Both the engineer and the artist within have a passion for clever techniques, particularly seamless construction and careful shaping. Finally (and there is nothing specifically Irish about this), I am inspired by all those who dream up new things to do with yarn and who experiment and play with this wonderful material. In other words, the knitter in me wants to have fun.

All these aspects of Irish heritage, and of my personal passions, come together in these patterns to create a book on Irish knitting as you've never before seen.

Getting the Most Out of This Book

The unique beauty of knitting your own garment is that you can make it fit *you*. The shoulders can be just the right size, the waist shaping can be in exactly the right position, and you can make the length just right for your body. Most importantly, you don't need to be afraid of making a pattern uniquely your own. The pattern is just the starting point; you should feel comfortable changing it to suit your own needs.

Modifying a simple pattern is not difficult to do if the knitted fabric itself is simple. However, when you are working with designs that use more complex stitch patterns, customizing a pattern requires a bit more care and forethought. Cabled stitch patterns are beautiful to look at (and fun to knit), but oftentimes produce very bulky fabrics. By using these stitch patterns selectively and taking care with their placement, you can retain the essence of a cabled design (like an Aran design) without creating as much weight and density. With innovative combinations, cabled stitch patterns can actually flatter the wearer. If possible, the underarm section should have a simple pattern that allows you to work increases and decreases in this area to actually shape your knit.

In this section, I have outlined some general guidelines to help you produce a finished item that fits perfectly and that you will treasure and wear for many years. Because most of the patterns in this book include traditional cable patterns, I have also included a final section detailing how to read the cable charts in this book. These pointers will help you make appropriate sizing decisions as you work with the patterns in this book, all of which are designed to create fitted, shaped garments rather than the knitted Aran "boxes" of the past!

Setting the Right Fit

Getting the right fit is of vital importance. If you want to love and wear your knitted item often, then you need to ensure that it fits well so that it is comfortable and flattering. If you knit your sweater too tightly, then it will be uncomfortable to wear and unattractive; if it's too loose, then it will become shapeless and baggy.

These 3 rules are the key to getting a good fit:

1. Know your swatch size.
2. Know your body size.
3. Know the finished size you want to knit.

Know Your Swatch Size

Start with a generously sized swatch (try for approximately a 6 × 6"/15 × 15 cm square). Measure it before you block it, and then wash and block the swatch. Gently pin the swatch to lie flat without stretching excessively. Allow it to dry fully. Now pick up your swatch, flop it around a little, and then let it settle naturally without stretching the fabric. Now measure the size of your swatch again. Don't try to push or pull the size; you need to get an honest measure. Ask yourself whether you like the fabric it produces. If your swatch is too loose and floppy, try a smaller needle. If the fabric is stiff and unyielding, then use a larger needle size. Also, check to see if the gauge is correct for the garment you're knitting. If you have more stitches per inch/cm than required, try a larger needle size. If you have too few stitches, try a smaller needle.

If you are not getting the correct gauge for the pattern, then you should knit swatches using different needle sizes until the gauge is correct. Alternatively, you may want to try swatching with a different yarn that might have a better chance of success. Even small differences in gauge from that suggested in a pattern can make a dramatic difference in the size of the garment.

Know Your Body Size

Before knitting a garment, make sure you take careful body measurements to ensure that you know your (or the intended recipient's) size. Start by measuring your key dimensions. These are your shoulder width, full bust circumference, waist circumference, and hip circumference (as shown in the diagram on the next page). You may also try to get someone to help you measure from the nape (back) of your neck to the center point of your waist. You should refer to these measurements when you are making decisions about sizing. After you determine the amount of ease that you want in your finished garment (see the "Ease" sidebar), then you can compare your size to the sizes on the pattern's schematic.

Measuring Tips:

When measuring your bust size, use the largest measurement around your chest.

Tie a piece of string around your waist and use this as a reference point to measure from the back of your neck. (See the body measurements diagram on the next page.)

Know the Finished Size You Want to Knit

Determining the finished size that you want to knit is actually more difficult than it sounds! You are used to walking into a shop, picking up a garment in your "size," and never actually stopping to think about the actual dimensions of the finished piece. How a garment fits you is determined by the amount of ease (see the "Ease" sidebar) in the finished piece.

How Much Ease Do You Need?

The answer to this question depends on your body type, personal preference, and the type of project you are working. For a very lightweight yarn worked in plain stockinette stitch, or for a smooth pattern, you

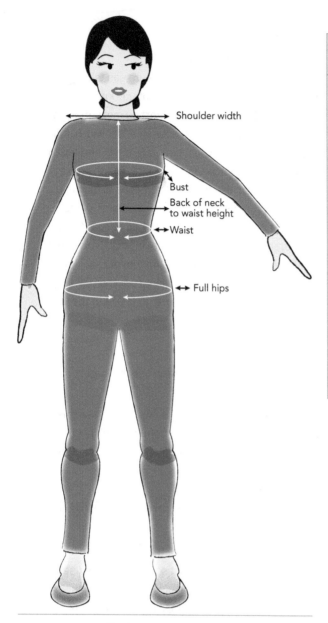

Body measurements

Ease

- 🍀 **Positive ease** is when the dimensions of the garment are larger than the dimensions of the person wearing it. If a person with a 34" (86cm) chest circumference is wearing a garment that measures 36" (91.5cm) around the chest, then the garment has 2 inches of *positive* ease.

- 🍀 **Negative ease** means that the size of the knitted garment is smaller than the dimensions of the person's body. The same woman with a 34" (86cm) bust might wear a fitted T-shirt that measures 32" around. This T-shirt has 2 inches of *negative* ease.

You should always bear in mind the recipient of the finished garment. Personal preferences and how it will be used can have a big impact on size choice. A jacket is usually worn over a shirt or sweater, so this will also need to be taken into account by providing extra room with a larger sized jacket. A good way of estimating the amount of ease to use in your knitting is by comparing your body measurements to a favorite garment. Make sure that the garment type is similar in weight and style to what you are planning on knitting. This will let you know how much ease you like to wear in a garment. Take note of whether it is loose fitting (positive ease) or snug fitting (negative ease).

All garment patterns in this book list two sets of dimensions: "Size" and "Finished Measurements." *The difference between these two measurements is my suggested ease for that garment.* Knitting patterns

can work with very little to no ease (or perhaps some negative ease). If the yarn you are using is thicker and you are using a denser stitch pattern, then the material itself will start to take up more room. It will also be stiffer with less stretch, so you might need several inches of positive ease.

Labels in illustration: Shoulder width, Bust, Back of neck to waist height, Waist, Full hips

are not always presented in this way; oftentimes, only the finished sizes are listed for the knitter. However, I prefer to show it this way in order to give knitters some idea of what size to knit for their dimensions. Please combine this suggestion with your own personal preference, so you will be happy with the end product.

I deliberately omitted generic sizing (XS, S, M, L) as these terms are oftentimes misleading. It is much more important for a knitter to use real measurements for garments to ensure a pefect fit for their size.

Who Are You Knitting For?
Knitting for Women

Traditional Aran knits are worked with little to no shaping, oftentimes not even at the shoulders (resulting in a drop-shoulder construction). Although this makes working intricate cable patterns easier (because you do not have to work decreases in the pattern), it creates a less-than-flattering garment to wear. To avoid this, follow these suggestions, which will help you produce a flattering finished item that you will want to wear again and again.

Waist Shaping   Unlike a traditional Aran sweater, most of the women's garments in this book decrease stitches at the waist to accentuate the natural curves of a woman's body. With waist shaping you need to be aware of two measurements: (1) *the nape-to-waist measurement* (discussed previously) to check the waist placement; and (2) *your waist size* (with desired ease) to determine the number of stitches you want at the waist. It can take some calculation to resize and reposition the waist of a knitted garment, but the standard waist shaping and position shown in this book's patterns should work well for most body types. However, if you know you have a high/low waist or a large/small waist, it may be worth your while to do these calculations.

If you do need to change the waist shaping for your size, use the schematic as a guide. Determine the number of rows you need to work to reach your desired waist placement and the number of stitches you want at your waist for your size. If you wish to read about shaping your own knits in more detail, a book such as *Sweater Design in Plain English,* by Maggie Righetti, is a great place to start.

Types of Shoulder Shaping

- **Raglan Shoulders:** Sleeves and body stitches all continue right up to the neckline. There are four defined decrease points (two for each shoulder), with body and sleeve stitches decreasing in a straight line every other row on each side of these predetermined lines. See the Ballinagree (Boy's Sweater) pattern for an example.

- **Saddle Shoulders:** A narrow strip of sleeve stitches continues up along the top of the shoulder (usually a few inches wide) on each side of the neck. The remaining armhole stitches are either shaped or abruptly stop. See the Knockmore (Men's Twisted Stitch Sweater) pattern for an example.

- **Set-in Shoulders:** Set-in shoulders are a more tailored style of shoulder shaping. The armhole is curved to follow the shape of the body and the sleeve cap is curved at the top to fit neatly into the armhole. See the Killorglin (Women's Cable Rib Jacket) pattern for an example.

Well-fitted Shoulders   The beauty of knitting your own garment is that you have the luxury of fitting the garment to your size. *Raglan shoulders* start at the neck and flow into the arms. *Set-in shoulders* and *saddle shoulders* fit the exact dimensions of your shoulders. (See the sidebar for more detail on shoulder shaping.) You may want to use a measurement that is slightly smaller than your true shoulder size because knitted fabric stretches a good deal. If you study where the top of set-in sleeves hits the tip of your shoulder blade, you may find that it is more flattering if it is set back from the tip of your shoulder a little.

Knitting for Children

In general, children grow upward faster than they grow outward. Keeping this in mind, use a few inches of positive ease for the body of a knitted garment, but keep the edgings snug so that the sleeves and hem will stay in place.

Typically, knits for girls will have a little less ease than boys. For girls' garments, 2–4" (5–10cm) of positive ease is typical, whereas 3–5" (7.5–12.5cm) of positive ease is usual for boys' garments.

Knitting for Men

Knitting for men is often very different than knitting for women. Typically, men prefer to wear a loose, classic-fitting garment that provides lots of movement and space. Take this into account when choosing a size to knit for a man. After measuring his chest size, see how much ease he typically likes in his sweaters and take it into account when choosing a size to knit. Oftentimes 4–6" (10–15cm) of positive ease are incorporated in men's knits. Remember to keep the waists and cuffs fitted, as with children's knits, so the garment doesn't hang off the body.

working with charts

Charts are used extensively in the patterns throughout this book. In fact, most cable patterns in this book are presented only in chart form. But fear not, charts are easier to read than you might think! Charts are a great way of illustrating pattern stitches, especially when you are working with cables. With a chart, you can immediately visualize what you are trying to create as well as see which stitches pass in front when you cross a cable. Working with charts makes it easier to read your knitting so that you can see where and when you have made a mistake.

If you have not used a chart before, you may be pleasantly surprised by how simple they are to use. When working in rows, you will read the chart from right to left on right-side (RS) rows. Also, right-side rows show the row numbers along the right side of the chart. When working a wrong-side (WS) row, you will read the row from left to right. The numbers for the wrong-side rows (if shown) are along the left side of the chart. Wrong-side row numbers are sometimes not shown on charts for clarity. All the patterns in this book, however, show both right- and left-side rows. If a pattern is worked in the round, then *every* row is a right-side row, so you will read every chart row from right to left and each row is numbered on the right side of the chart.

Charts have a legend that lets you know what each symbol represents. Before you begin knitting, note how stitches are worked depending on whether you are on the right or wrong side of the work. For example, stockinette stitch is knit on the right side, but purled on the wrong side.

A few simple things will help you prevent mistakes when working with charts. To begin with, make a photocopy of your chart. You can even enlarge the chart, which will make it easier to read. For more complex stitches, use a highlighter to mark all the symbols of the same type so they will jump out at you and be easier to spot. For instance, highlighting all four-stitch left cables in green and highlighting all four-stitch right cables in pink will let you see at a glance which way to turn the cable. A sticky note or sheet of paper is also a great tool to use. Simply place the sticky note or paper above the row you are working and you will never accidently work the wrong row of the chart, even if you get distracted from your knitting.

With all of the preceding pointers on fit, ease, and sizing you now have the tools to knit a great-fitting garment for yourself or your recipient. If you follow these steps, you won't be disappointed with your end result and you'll eliminate any surprises along the way! So just to briefly recap the steps:

1. Measure yourself (or your recipient) accurately.
2. Choose the correct style of garment to suit the wearer.
3. Choose the correct size from the pattern to knit.
4. The most important step is to make a gauge swatch (and block your swatch!) before you knit, so you are certain that your knitted size will match the schematic.

Enjoy the patterns in this book, and have lots of fun knitting and experimenting!

kerry woollen mills

Andrew Eadie's family has been running the Kerry Woollen Mills for over 100 years—and the mills themselves began operating over 300 years ago. But even within his own lifetime, he has seen dramatic changes in the business. He can remember a time not too long ago when his mill would "deliver 20–30kg (44–66 lbs.) of wool to Cleary's (a shop in Dublin) every day—when everyone hand knit their own jumpers (sweaters)." Although this volume of yarn sales no longer exists, the mill still produces high-quality yarn from its small mill situated by the river Gweestin, a few miles outside Killarney near the village of Beaufort.

I began my visit to the mills by spending some time in the cozy warmth of the mill shop, where every wall is covered from floor to ceiling with shelves bending under the weight of jumpers, capes, caps, mittens, and blankets. But it was the yarn that brought me here—specifically the organic yarn that makes the Kerry Woollen Mills unique in Ireland. The mill buys fleece from certified organic sources around Ireland—including Tipperary, Wexford, Cavan, Mullingar, and Galway—and uses it to create yarn both for sale and for use in their own line of garments and textiles. But sourcing organic fleece in Ireland is not easy; the

wool must come from a certified organic farm that does not use chemical pesticides on the land or animals. For the most part, wool fleece is only a by-product of the organic meat industry in Ireland, rather than a profitable product in its own right. This means a large supply is not available, particularly in darker natural colors. (The organic yarns are not dyed, so any color variations are entirely due to the type of fleece used.) As a result, the mill spins the darker Jacob* wool fleece into fingering-weight yarn and uses this organic yarn to produce their own exclusive line of sweaters, hats, scarves, and gloves. The only organic, Aran-weight yarn they sell for use in hand knitting comes in white.

NOTE: Jacob is a sheep breed that produces a naturally brown-colored fleece. Depending on the sheep, this color varies between a dark and light shade. Fleece is sorted into different grades of color to produce natural undyed color variations.

Because the supply of organic fleece is sporadic, the mill's organic yarn is not always available. Fortunately, their standard Aran-weight yarn is always in stock. The fleece used for their standard Aran-weight yarn is from a mixture of Irish and New Zealand

Rolls of slubbing waiting to be spun.

fleeces. Irish sheep fleece tends to be quite yellow, so it is blended with whiter New Zealand fleece to create a whiter end product.

After providing a brief overview about the sourcing of the mill's organic yarn, Andrew led me down a cobble-stoned path and into a building that has been in use for over three centuries. Inside are rows of heavy machinery, busily transforming piles of fleece into yarn. The whole experience is new to me—although I know a great deal about knitting, I have never looked closely at the process used to make the yarns that I know and love. And what a process it is!

First, mountains of fluffy fleece are placed in a huge hopper for *carding* (see sidebar). The fleece is then pulled through the *carder,* which is a series of rollers covered in kinked wire teeth that move the fleece from one roller to another until the fibers are loose. These fibers are then scraped off by the *doffer* (see sidebar) and passed along to the *Scotch Intermediate Feed* (see sidebar), which has finer teeth that are used to change the direction of the fibers. This process creates the random fiber orientation needed to create the characteristic "airiness" of *woolen spun* yarn (see sidebar).

Next, the carded wool is split into several strands that are rolled in a "condenser," which draws out and slightly twists the strands to create the *slubbing*. The slubbing (*see photo*), which is composed of lightly twisted strands, already looks like yarn, but when you handle it you discover it has no strength yet; it just falls apart. This is where the spinning comes into play. The slubbing is wound onto large bobbins and loaded onto the spinning machine, called a *mule.* Pulling from many bobbins at the same time, the machine twists the slubbing quickly to add strength and create the finished yarn. (If you've never spun, or seen it done, you can see for yourself how this works: simply create a twisted cord and watch how the yarn twists around itself, thus creating a stronger twisted material.)

Streams provide essential clean water for processing the yarn.

Some of the yarn will finish its journey (just as I finished my tour) with a visit to the dyeing room and its large stainless steel vats. When dyeing finished material or yarn, a machine draws the material or yarn through the water and dye. Yarn with one solid color is generally carded and spun in its natural state and then dyed after it has become yarn, thus creating a more consistent pigmentation. However, not all yarn is dyed at the *end* of the process. In many cases, the fleece is dyed *before* the whole carding, slubbing, and spinning process begins. In this situation, a different machine is used to drive the water and dye *through* the material rather than the other way around. The pre-dyeing of fleece is often used to produce yarns with subtle color variations and a tweed effect.

Finally, some of the wool will never see the dyeing room at all. Natural yarns are not dyed, but instead

Woolen Spun Yarn

Fibers are combed in a random orientation which creates a more airy yarn that is generally used in hand knitting. The yarn that is spun at Kerry Woollen Mills uses this method.

Yarn Review

Kerry Woollen Mills "Aran Wool"

Weight: 200g (350 yd./320m)
Material: 100% wool
Needle Size: US 8 (5mm)
Gauge: 17 sts × 23 rows = 4" (10cm) in St st

When picking up the generously sized hank of this yarn, my first impression was the strong, rich smell of natural lanolin. While winding the yarn into balls, I also noticed a certain amount of stickiness, which makes this yarn particularly good for projects that involve steeking. The yarn knitted up quickly and evenly into a firm fabric. As with most Irish wool, the yarn has a slightly rough texture, but after washing the swatch, the fabric softened well and draped nicely. For durable outerwear projects, this yarn provides tremendous value for the money and will last for years.

NOTE: *For spinners, carded wool is also available from Kerry Woollen Mills.*

A selection of yarns sold in the mill shop.

retain the natural color of the sheep's fleece. The natural colors of Jacob sheep, for example, vary widely and "light Jacob," "mid Jacob," and "dark Jacob" describe the different fleece colors of this sheep breed.

In the end, I came away from the Kerry Woollen Mills with a lot of new knowledge, a deeper appreciation for the process of creating yarn, and, most of all, an itch to start knitting with the wonderful yarn I brought home with me.

NOTE: *For information on where to buy Kerry Woollen Mills yarns, please refer to the "Yarn Availability and Substitutions" appendix.*

Worsted Spun Yarn

Fibers are combed in parallel to create *worsted spun yarn,* which is smoother, stronger, and well suited to rugs, blankets, and other hard-wearing items. Many of the mill's woven items, such as blankets and throws, use worsted spun yarn that is imported. However, Kerry Woollen Mills does not use this spinning method when producing its own yarn.

killorslin

Women's Cable Rib Jacket

This slim-fitting ribbed jacket uses interwoven ribs on the front and back to create a sophisticated and complicated-looking jacket, but with minimal fuss. A high collar is great for winter warmth and the zipper closure finishes the piece very neatly.

size

To fit actual bust circumference up to: 31 (34, 38, 41, 45, 48, 52)"/78.5 (86.5, 96.5, 104, 114.5, 122, 132) cm

0–2" (0–5cm) of positive ease is recommended.

finished measurements

Bust circumference: 31 (34.5, 38, 41.5, 45.25, 48.75, 52.25)"/78.5 (87.5, 96.5, 105.5, 115, 124, 133) cm
Length: 20.5 (21, 21.5, 22, 22.5, 23, 23.5)"/52 (53.5, 54.5, 56, 57, 58.5, 59.5) cm

Size 34.5" (87.5cm) modeled with no ease.

materials

- Kerry Woollen Mills "Aran Wool" (100% wool; 350 yd./320m per 200g skein); Color: Petrol; 3 (3, 4, 4, 5, 5, 6) skeins
- US 8 (5mm) double-pointed needles
- 2 sets US 8 (5mm) circular needles, 32" (80cm) length (or longer for larger sizes), *or size needed to obtain gauge*

  NOTE: *Second needle is used to hold back sts when working on front.*
- US 7 (4.5mm) double-pointed needles
- US 7 (4.5mm) circular needle, 32" (80cm) length (or longer for larger sizes)
- Cable needle
- Tapestry needle
- Stitch markers
- Waste yarn
- Stitch holder
- Zipper, 20 (20, 20, 20, 22, 22, 22)"/51 (51, 51, 51, 56, 56, 56) cm length

gauge

18 sts × 24 rows = 4" (10cm) in 3 × 1 Ribbing on larger needles

41 sts of Medallion Chart and Ribbed Cable Chart measures 7.5" (19cm) across

pattern notes

For m1, backwards loop cast-on, provisional cast-on, and short row (w&t) techniques, please see the "Knitting Techniques" appendix.

3 × 1 Ribbing (rows)
(worked over a multiple of 4 sts + 1)

RS: *P1, k3; rep from * to last st, p1.

WS: *K1, p3; rep from* to last st, k1.

3 × 1 Ribbing (rnds)

(worked over a multiple of 4 sts)

All Rnds: *P1, k3; rep from * to end of rnd.

Medallion Chart

Worked over 41 sts; see chart for details.

Ribbed Cable Chart

Worked on front of jacket and lower back over 41 sts. Note that blue highlighted cables are different for right and left sides; details given in legend.

Sleeve Cable Chart

Worked on sleeves over 25 sts. Note that blue highlighted cables are different for right and left sleeves; details given in legend.

Instructions

This jacket is worked from the top down. Starting with a provisional cast-on, you will work short rows across the back to form the shoulders and to shape the neck. Then you will work the front from the provisional cast-on. When you reach the underarm, you will work the body in one piece to the bottom. Set-in sleeves are worked from the top, shaping the sleeve cap with short rows at the top.

shoulders
Back Shoulders

With larger circular needle, CO 57 (57, 65, 65, 73, 81) sts using provisional cast-on.

Work 2 rows in 3 × 1 Ribbing.

Next Row (RS): Work in 3 × 1 Ribbing for 16 (16, 16, 16, 16, 20, 20) sts, pm for neck, work 25 (25, 33, 33, 33, 33, 41) sts, pm for neck, work 4 sts, w&t.

Next Row (WS): Work in patt to second marker, work 4 more sts, w&t.

Next Row: Work in patt to wrapped st, pick up wrap and work it together with the wrapped st, work 3 sts more, w&t.

Rep last row until all sts have been worked, ending with a WS row. Pick up any rem wraps as they are passed. Remove neck markers.

Work 8 (8, 12, 12, 12, 16, 20) sts in 3 × 1 Ribbing, pm, work Medallion Chart over next 41 sts, pm, work to end of row in 3 × 1 Ribbing as set.

NOTE: The Medallion Chart is worked across the marked 41 sts until all 40 rows are complete. When Medallion Chart is complete, continue with Ribbed Cable Chart across these 41 sts until the back is complete.

Continue working in est'd patt until armhole measures 4 (3.5, 4, 3.5, 3, 3.5, 3.75)"/10 (9, 10, 9, 7.5, 9, 9.5) cm (measured from outside edge of shoulder) ending on a WS row.

Armhole Shaping

NOTE: Keeping the first and last sts as selvedge sts, work the m1 increases as purls or knits to maintain 3 × 1 Ribbing patt.

*Next Row (RS): P1, m1, work in patt to last st, m1, p1.

Next Row (WS): Work in patt.

Rep these 2 rows 5 (7, 7, 9, 11, 11, 11) more times.

Next Row (RS): P1, m1, work in patt to last st, m1, p1.

Next Row (WS): K1, m1, work in patt to last st, m1, k1.

Rep the last 2 rows 0 (1, 1, 1, 2, 2, 2) time(s).* 73 (81, 89, 93, 101, 109, 117) sts.

Break yarn and set sts aside. Make note of last row worked on chart.

front. Attach second ball of yarn, work in 3 × 1 Ribbing across left front.

Instructions for both fronts are given below. When instructions differ between the right front and left front, they will be divided by a semicolon (;).

Next Row (WS): Work in patt.

Next Row (RS): Work right front sts; work 4 left front sts, w&t.

Next Row (WS): Work left front sts; work 4 right front sts, w&t.

Continue to work short rows (w&t), working 4 more sts on each side before turning until all sts have been worked on each side. Take care to pick up wraps and work them together with the sts they wrap as you pass them.

Neck Shaping

NOTE: Work the m1 increases as purls or knits to maintain 3 × 1 Ribbing patt.

Working 1 st in from edge, increase 1 st at each edge using m1 increases every RS row at neck edge on both fronts 6 (6, 8, 8, 6, 6, 6) times and then *every* row 4 (4, 5, 5, 6, 6, 9) times. 26 (26, 29, 29, 28, 32, 35) sts on each side.

Work 0 (0, 1, 1, 0, 0, 1) WS row.

Next Row (RS): Work in patt across right front, CO 7 (7, 8, 8, 9, 9, 10) sts using backwards loop cast-on at neck edge; CO 7 (7, 8, 8, 9, 9, 10) sts using backwards loop cast-on at neck edge, work in patt across left front. 33 (33, 37, 37, 37, 41, 45) sts each side.

Next Row (WS): Work in 3 × 1 Ribbing to last 4 sts of left side, p4; p4, work in 3 × 1 Ribbing to end.

NOTE: There are not enough sts to complete the Ribbed Cable Chart for all sizes. Work incomplete chart as described below, omitting cables if there are not enough sts to work them.

Front Shoulders

The two fronts are worked simultaneously from the shoulders down using two balls of yarn.

Undo provisional cast-on, and place first 16 (16, 16, 16, 16, 20, 20) sts on large circular needle, place central 25 (25, 33, 33, 33, 33, 41) sts on holder for back neck, place final 16 (16, 16, 16, 16, 20, 20) sts on same circular needle.

With RS facing, attach yarn, work in 3 × 1 Ribbing (ensure ribbing matches with back sts) across right

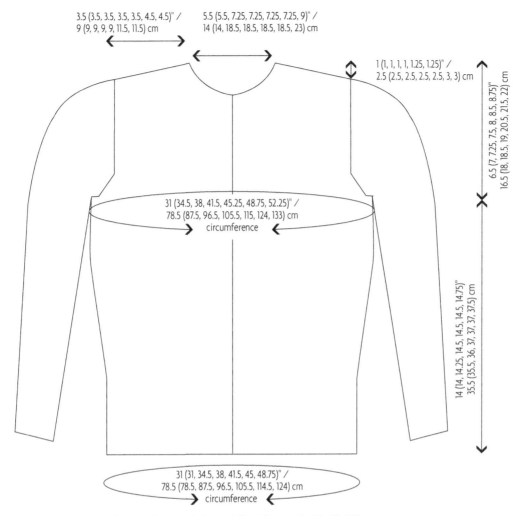

3.5 (3.5, 3.5, 3.5, 3.5, 4.5, 4.5)" / 9 (9, 9, 9, 9, 11.5, 11.5) cm

5.5 (5.5, 7.25, 7.25, 7.25, 7.25, 9)" / 14 (14, 18.5, 18.5, 18.5, 18.5, 23) cm

1 (1, 1, 1, 1, 1.25, 1.25)" / 2.5 (2.5, 2.5, 2.5, 2.5, 3, 3) cm

6.5 (7, 7.25, 7.5, 8, 8.5, 8.75)" / 16.5 (18, 18.5, 19, 20.5, 21.5, 22) cm

31 (34.5, 38, 41.5, 45.25, 48.75, 52.25)" / 78.5 (87.5, 96.5, 105.5, 115, 124, 133) cm circumference

14 (14, 14.25, 14.5, 14.5, 14.5, 14.75)" 35.5 (35.5, 36, 37, 37, 37, 37.5) cm

31 (31, 34.5, 38, 41.5, 45, 48.75)" / 78.5 (78.5, 87.5, 96.5, 105.5, 114.5, 124) cm circumference

Sleeve length: 18 (18.5, 18.5, 19, 19, 19.5, 19.5)"/45.5 (47, 47, 48.5, 48.5, 49.5, 49.5) cm
Upper arm circ.: 12.5 (12.5, 14.25, 14.25, 16, 16, 16)"/31.5 (31.5, 36, 36, 40.5, 40.5, 40.5) cm
Wrist circ.: 9 (9, 10.75, 10.75, 10.75, 10.75, 10.75)"/22.5 (22.5, 27, 27, 27, 27, 27) cm

Next Row (RS): Work Ribbed Cable Chart [starting on st 13 (13, 9, 9, 9, 5, 1) of chart], sl 1, k3; k3, sl 1, work Ribbed Cable Chart substituting c3 over 4 right for the highlighted cables (starting on st 1 of chart). (NOTE: You will not yet be able to complete the chart for all sizes).

Next Row (WS): On left front, work Ribbed Cable Chart using c3 over 4 right for the highlighted cables to last 4 sts, p4; p4, work Ribbed Cable Chart using c3 over 4 left for the highlighted cables to end of row.

Continue working in est'd patt until armhole measures 4 (3.5, 4, 3.5, 3, 3.5, 3.75)"/10 (9, 10, 9, 7.5, 9, 9.5) cm.

Armhole Shaping

Work armhole shaping from * to * as for back, working inc'd sts into Ribbed Cable Chart and working sts outside the chart in 3 × 1 Ribbing. 41 (45, 49, 51, 55, 59, 63) sts each side.

Break yarn from right front.

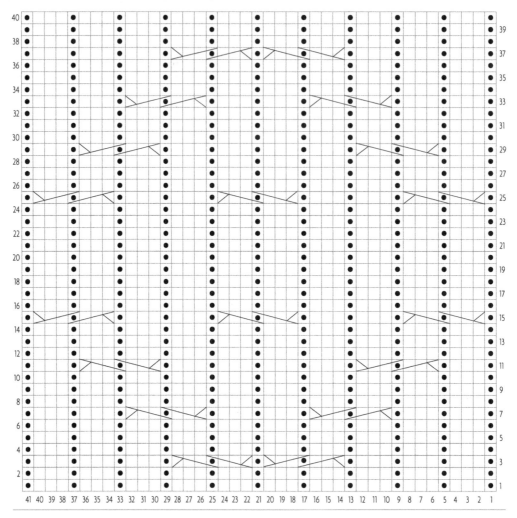

Medallion Chart

body

With RS facing, work left front in patt, CO 7 (7, 7, 11, 11, 11, 11) sts using backwards loop cast-on method, work back sts in patt, CO 7 (7, 7, 11, 11, 11, 11) sts using backwards loop method, work right front in patt. 169 (185, 201, 217, 233, 249, 265) sts.

Position Side Markers (WS): Incorporating newly cast-on sts into 3 × 1 Ribbing patt, work 44 (48, 52, 56, 60, 64, 68) sts, pm, work to last 44 (48, 52, 56, 60, 64, 68) sts, pm, work to end of row.

Work in est'd patt until body measures 2" (5cm) from underarm, ending with a WS row.

Smallest Size (31.75"/80.5cm)

Smallest size (31.75"/80.5cm) has **no** waist shaping. Work in patt until body measures 11" (28cm) from underarm. Then proceed with instructions under "All Sizes."

All Other Sizes

Waist Dec Row (RS): *Work to 2 sts before side m, ssk, sm, p1, k2tog, work to 3 sts before next side m, ssk, p1, sm, k2tog, work to end of row.

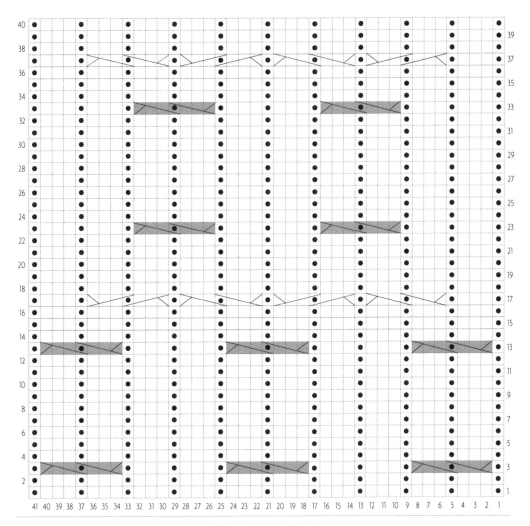

Ribbed Cable Chart

Work Waist Dec Row every 12 rnds 3 more times. 153 (169, 185, 201, 217, 233, 249) sts.

Work in patt until body measures (11, 11.25, 11.5, 11.5, 11.5, 11.75)"/(28, 28.5, 29, 29, 29, 30) cm from underarm.

All Sizes

Change to smaller circular needle, and work in 3 × 1 Ribbing for 3" (7.5cm).

BO all sts in patt.

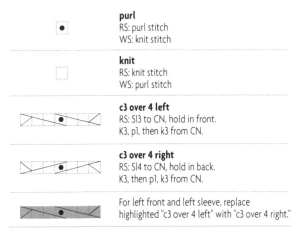

	purl RS: purl stitch WS: knit stitch
	knit RS: knit stitch WS: purl stitch
	c3 over 4 left RS: Sl3 to CN, hold in front. K3, p1, then k3 from CN.
	c3 over 4 right RS: Sl4 to CN, hold in back. K3, then p1, k3 from CN.
	For left front and left sleeve, replace highlighted "c3 over 4 left" with "c3 over 4 right."

Legend to Medallion and Ribbed Cable Charts

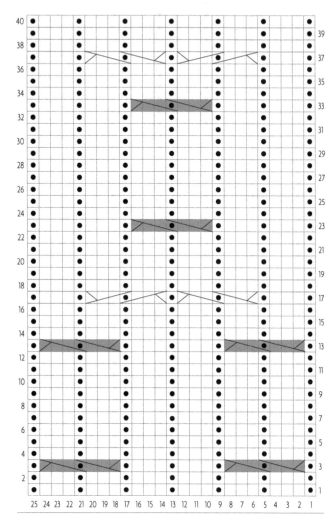

Sleeve Cable Chart

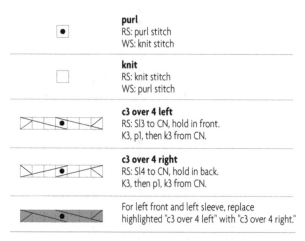

purl
RS: purl stitch
WS: knit stitch

knit
RS: knit stitch
WS: purl stitch

c3 over 4 left
RS: Sl3 to CN, hold in front.
K3, p1, then k3 from CN.

c3 over 4 right
RS: Sl4 to CN, hold in back.
K3, then p1, k3 from CN.

For left front and left sleeve, replace
highlighted "c3 over 4 left" with "c3 over 4 right."

Legend to Sleeve Cable Chart

sleeves
Short-row Sleeve Cap

With RS facing and larger dpns, begin at the center of the underarm CO sts, pick up knit 4 (4, 4, 6, 6, 6, 6) sts from CO sts, pick up and knit 24 (24, 28, 26, 30, 30, 30) sts evenly up side of armhole to top of sleeve cap, pm for center of sleeve cap, pick up and knit 25 (25, 29, 27, 31, 31, 31) sts evenly down side of armhole, pick up and knit 3 (3, 3, 5, 5, 5, 5) sts from

rem CO underarm sts, pm for start of rnd. 56 (56, 64, 64, 72, 72, 72) sts.

Next Row (RS): Work in 3 × 1 Ribbing to 4 (4, 5, 5, 6, 6, 6) sts past sleeve cap center m, w&t.

Next Row (WS): Work 8 (8, 10, 10, 12, 12, 12) sts in patt, w&t.

Next Row: Work in patt to wrapped st, pick up wrap and work it together with the wrapped st, wrap next st, turn.

Rep last row until only 3 (3, 3, 5, 5, 5, 5) sts rem unworked on each side of the *underarm* marker.

Work complete rnd in patt, picking up any rem wraps and removing sleeve cap marker.

Arm
NOTE: *When working Sleeve Cable Chart in the rnd, read all rows from right to left.*

Work 16 (16, 20, 20, 24, 24, 24) sts in patt, pm, work Sleeve Cable Chart, pm, work in 3 × 1 Ribbing to end of rnd. You will continue with Sleeve Cable Chart, ***noting chart difference between right and left sleeve cables,*** between markers until you reach the cuff.

Work 10 (10, 10, 10, 6, 7, 7) rnds in patt.

Sleeve Dec Rnd: P1, k2tog, work in patt to last 2 sts, ssk.

Rep these 11 (11, 11, 11, 7, 8, 8) rnds 6 (3, 3, 0, 0, 9, 9) times more.

Then work Sleeve Dec Rnd every 12 (12, 12, 12, 8, 9, 9) rnds 1 (4, 4, 7, 11, 2, 2) times. 40 (40, 48, 48, 48, 48) sts.

Cont in est'd patt until sleeve measures 15 (15.5, 15.5, 16, 16, 16.5, 16.5)"/ 38 (39.5, 39.5, 40.5, 40.5, 42, 42) cm from underarm.

Change to smaller dpns and work in 3 × 1 Ribbing for 3" (7.5cm).

BO all sts in patt loosely.

Rep for second sleeve.

Finishing

collar

With smaller circular needle and RS facing, begin at the cast-on neck sts on right neck and pick up and knit 24 (24, 30, 30, 30, 30, 32) sts evenly up to shoulder, work 25 (25, 33, 33, 33, 33, 41) held sts for back neck, pick up and knit 24 (24, 30, 30, 30, 30, 32) sts down left side of neck. 73 (73, 93, 93, 93, 93, 105) sts.

Next Row (WS): P4, work in 3 × 1 Ribbing (WS row) until last 4 sts, p4.

Next Row (RS): K3, sl 1, work in 3 × 1 Ribbing until last 4 sts, sl 1, k3.

Cont working in est'd patt until collar measures 2" (5cm), ending with a WS row.

Next Row (RS): K2tog, k1, sl 1, work in patt to last 4 sts, sl 1, k1, k2tog. 71 (71, 91, 91, 91, 91, 103) sts.

Next Row (WS): P3, work in patt to last 3 sts, p3.

Next Row (RS): K2tog, sl 1, work in patt to last 4 sts, sl 1, k2tog. 69 (69, 89, 89, 89, 89, 101) sts.

Next Row (WS): P2, work in patt to last 2 sts, p2.

Next Row (RS): K2tog, work in patt to last 2 sts, k2tog. 67 (67, 87, 87, 87, 87, 99) sts.

Next Row (WS): Sl 1, work in patt to last st, p1.

Next Row (RS): Sl 1, work in patt to last st, k1.

Rep last 2 rows until collar measures 4" (10cm) from picked up sts.

BO all sts in patt.

zipper

Fold hem to WS along slipped st line on both sides of front and sew in place.

Attach zipper to WS, so that the zipper bands just touch.

Fold the collar down, fitting top of zipper inside the fold to prevent the zipper's edge from rubbing neck when worn. Sew edge of collar to inside along line of picked up sts.

Weave in all yarn ends with tapestry needle.

Block gently to dimensions given on schematic.

Tralee (Women's Aran Skirt)

Tralee

Women's Aran Skirt

The creamy natural texture of Kerry Woollen Mills' organic yarn is showcased beautifully with this sleek skirt. Figure hugging to the knee, the kick pleats on each side hide a little Aran detailing that provides lots of extra room for leg movement.

Knit in the round from the bottom up, you can customize the length of this skirt to suit your figure because it's easy to add extra length if you need it. Worked in a lighter yarn to reduce bulk, the simplicity of the design allows you to knit this skirt very quickly.

size

To fit actual waist circumference up to: 23.75 (27.5, 31.75, 35.5, 39, 44, 47.75)"/60.5 (70, 80.5, 90, 99, 112, 121.5) cm

finished measurements

Waist: 24.75 (28.5, 32.75, 36.5, 40, 45, 48.75)"/63 (72, 83, 92.5, 101.5, 114.5, 124) cm

Hips: 34.25 (38.5, 42.25, 45.75, 49.5, 53, 57.5)"/87 (98, 107, 116.5, 125.5, 135, 146) cm

Length: 23 (23.5, 23.75, 24, 24.5, 24.75, 25.25)"/58.5 (60, 60.5, 61, 62, 63, 64) cm

Size 28.5" (72cm) waist modeled on a 26.5" (67.5cm) waist. Choose a size 1–2" (2.5–5cm) larger than your natural waist.

materials

- Kerry Woollen Mills "Organic 2-ply" (100% wool; 490 yd./450m per 200g skein); Color: Natural; 2 (2, 2, 3, 3, 3, 4) skeins

  NOTE: *Black Water Abbey Yarns (available in the U.S.) stocks Kerry Woollen Mills' "2-ply Fingering Weight Wool" in an "Ecru" colorway that can be held double to substitute for the above yarn.*

- US 4 (3.5mm) circular needle, 40" (100cm) length (or longer for larger sizes), *or size needed to obtain gauge*
- US 4 (3.5mm) circular needle, 24" (60cm) length (or longer for larger sizes)
- Spare US 4 (3.5mm) double-pointed needles (to work pleats)
- Cable needle
- Tapestry needle
- Stitch markers
- 1" (2.5cm)-wide elastic, cut to your waist measurement

gauge

22 sts × 32 rows = 4" (10cm) in St st

pattern notes

For whipstitch instructions, please see the "Knitting Techniques" appendix.

Double Moss Stitch

*(worked in rnds over an **even number of sts**)*

Rnds 1 & 2: *K1, p1; rep from * to end of rnd.

Rnds 3 & 4: *P1, k1; rep from * to end of rnd.

Rep these 4 rnds for patt.

Double Moss Stitch

*(worked in rnds over an **odd number of sts**)*

Rnds 1 & 2: *K1, p1; rep from * to last st, k1.

Rnds 3 & 4: *P1, k1; rep from * to last st, p1.

Rep these 4 rnds for patt.

Pleat Cable

Worked over 39 sts; see chart for details.

Instructions

Knit from the bottom up in the round, the kick pleat at each side is created by slipping some sts to spare double-pointed needles, folding the fabric, and knitting the sts from the resulting three layers together.

edgins

With longer circular needle, CO 344 (368, 388, 408, 428, 448, 472) sts, join to work in the rnd taking care not to twist sts, and pm for start of rnd.

Rnd begins at center of back.

Set-Up Rnd: Work 47 (53, 57, 63, 67, 73, 79) sts in Double Moss St, sl 1, pm for start of pleat, work 77 sts in Double Moss St, pm for end of pleat, sl 1, work 93 (105, 115, 125, 135, 145, 157) sts in Double Moss St, sl 1, pm for start of pleat, work 77 sts in Double Moss St, pm for end of pleat, sl 1, work 46 (52, 58, 62, 68, 72, 78) sts in Double Moss St to end of rnd.

Rnd 1: *Work in Double Moss St to 1 st before m, k1, sm, work in Double Moss St to m, sm, k1; rep from * once, work in Double Moss St to end of rnd.

Rnd 2: *Work in Double Moss St to 1 st before m, sl 1, sm, work in Double Moss St to m, sm, sl 1; rep from * once, work in Double Moss St to end of rnd.

Rep Rnds 1 and 2 until edging measures 1" (2.5cm), ending with Rnd 1.

pleats

Rnd 1: *K to 11 sts before m, work 10 sts in Double Moss St, sl 1, sm, k19, work Pleat Cable Chart over 39 sts, k19, sm, sl 1, work 10 sts in Double Moss St; rep from *, k to end of rnd.

Rnd 2: *K to 11 sts before m, work 10 sts in Double Moss St, k1, sm, k19, work Pleat Cable Chart over 39 sts, k19, sm, k1, work 10 sts in Double Moss St; rep from *, k to end of rnd.

Work in est'd patt until work measures 7" (18cm) from CO edge.

close pleats

To close the pleats, you will slip groups of 19 sts to 2 dpns (dpn 1 and dpn 2), then fold the skirt into 3 overlapping layers of fabric with the cabled section at the back and the Double Moss St layer closest to you. Then, with those 3 needles held parallel in the left hand, you will knit the sts from all 3 needles together with the end of the circular needle in the right hand.

Next Rnd: *K to 19 sts before m; place next 19 sts on dpn 1, remove m, place next 19 sts on dpn 2, fold fabric so that dpn 2 is in front of the LH working needle (RS together), and dpn 1 is in front of dpn 2 (WS together), hold these 3 needles in the left hand and knit 1 st from each needle (3 sts) tog 8 times, working in Double Moss St, work 1 st from each needle (3 sts) tog 11 times (first half of pleat complete), k1 (or p1 to keep in patt); place next 19 sts on dpn 1, place following 19 sts on dpn 2, fold fabric so that dpn 2 is in front of dpn 1 (RS together), and LH working needle is in front of dpn 2 (WS together), working in

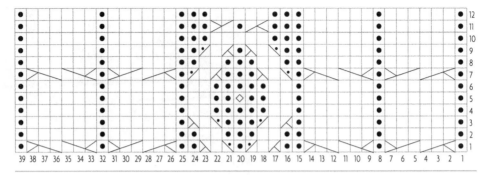

Pleat Cable Chart

purl		
●	purl stitch	
	c3 over 3 right	
	Sl3 to CN, hold in back.	
	K3, k3 from CN.	
	c3 over 3 left	
	Sl3 to CN, hold in front.	
	K3, k3 from CN.	
	c2 over 1 right P	
	Sl1 to CN, hold in back.	
	K2, p1 from CN.	
	c2 over 1 left P	
	Sl2 to CN, hold in front.	
	P1, k2 from CN.	
	knit	
	Knit stitch	
	bobble	
◇	To make bobble: (k1, p1) twice in one stitch, turn and p4. Turn and sl2-k2tog-pass 2 sl sts over, completing bobble.	
	c2 over 3 right	
	Sl3 to CN, hold in back. K2, then from CN sl final purl st to left needle and p, k2 from CN.	

Legend

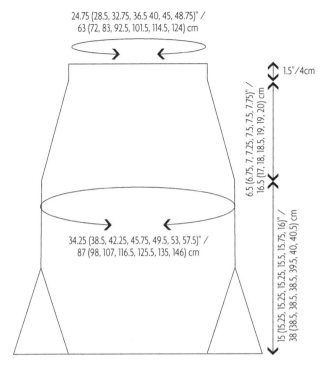

24.75 (28.5, 32.75, 36.5 40, 45, 48.75)" / 63 (72, 83, 92.5, 101.5, 114.5, 124) cm

1.5"/4cm

6.5 (6.75, 7, 7.25, 7.5, 7.5, 7.75)" / 16.5 (17, 18, 18.5, 19, 19, 20) cm

34.25 (38.5, 42.25, 45.75, 49.5, 53, 57.5)" / 87 (98, 107, 116.5, 125.5, 135, 146) cm

15 (15.25, 15.25, 15.25, 15.5, 15.75, 16)" / 38 (38.5, 38.5, 38.5, 39.5, 40, 40.5) cm

Double Moss St work 1 st from each needle (3 sts) tog 11 times, knit 1 st from each needle (3 sts) tog 8 times; rep from * for second kick pleat, knit to end of rnd—152 sts dec'd. 192 (216, 236, 256, 276, 296, 320) sts.

Place 4 markers for darts (dm), before and after the Double Moss St panels.

Dec Rnd: *K to dm, sm, work 10 sts in Double Moss St, k3tog (or p3tog to keep in patt), work 10 sts in Double Moss St, sm, rep from *, k to end of rnd—4 sts dec'd. 188 (212, 232, 252, 272, 292, 316) sts.

Work without shaping in est'd patt until work measures 15 (15.25, 15.25, 15.25, 15.5, 15.75, 16)"/38 (38.5, 38.5, 38.5, 39.5, 40, 40.5) cm from CO edge.

waist shaping

NOTE: *Change to shorter circular needle when necessary.*

Waist Dec Rnd: *Work to 2 sts before dm, k2tog, sm, work to dm, sm, ssk; rep from *, k to end of rnd—4 sts dec'd. 184 (208, 228, 248, 268, 288, 312) sts.

Work Waist Dec Rnd every 5 (5, 5, 5, 5, 6, 6) rnds 4 (2, 8, 10, 12, 10, 7) times and then every 4 (4, 4, 4, 0, 0, 5) rnds 8 (11, 4, 2, 0, 0, 4) times. 136 (156, 180, 200, 220, 248, 268) sts.

Work measures approx 21.5 (22, 22.25, 22.5, 23, 23.25, 23.75)"/54.5 (56, 56.5, 57, 58.5, 59, 60.5) cm.

waistband casing

Knit 10 rnds, purl 1 rnd, knit 10 rnds. Break yarn leaving very long tail to sew waistband in place.

Finishing
waistband

Cut elastic 1" (2.5cm) less than actual waist measurement. Sew ends together, with approx 1" (2.5cm) overlap.

Place elastic into waistband casing, fold casing to WS along purl row and whipstitch live sts to the WS at the first round of the waistband casing.

With tapestry needle, weave in all loose ends.

Block skirt to dimensions given on schematic.

Listowel (Girl's Heart Shrug)

liscowel

Girl's Heart Shrug

Your little girl will be warm and snug in this cozy shrug. Ideal to throw over a special dress, the warm aran-weight yarn is functional and attractive. A delicate heart, shaped using cables, will make her feel very special.

size

To fit actual chest circumference up to: 21 (23, 25, 27, 28)"/53.5 (58.5, 63.5, 68.5, 71) cm

Suggested ages: 2 (4, 6, 8, 10) years

0–1" (0–2.5cm) of positive ease is recommended.

finished measurements

Back width: 12.5 (13, 14, 14.75, 15.25)"/31.5 (33, 35.5, 37.5, 38.5) cm

NOTE: *You can measure back width by halving the chest circumference.*

Length: 5.5 (5.75, 6.5, 7, 7.25)"/14 (15, 16.5, 17.5, 18.5) cm

Shown in 12.5" (31.5cm) back width on a 2 year-old with 1" (2.5cm) of positive ease.

materials

- Kerry Woollen Mills "Aran Wool" (100% wool; 350 yd./320m per 200g skein); Color: Cerise; 1 (1, 2, 2, 2) skein(s)
- US 8 (5mm) straight needles, *or size needed to obtain gauge*
- US 8 (5mm) double-pointed needles
- US 7 (4.5mm) double-pointed needles
- US 7 (4.5mm) circular needle, 24" (60cm) length
- Cable needle
- Tapestry needle
- Stitch markers
- Waste yarn

gauge

17 sts × 22 rows = 4" (10cm) in St st on larger needles

pattern notes

For the m1 increase technique, please see the "Knitting Techniques" appendix.

Pfkb: Purl into front of stitch, knit into back of stitch.

Kfpb: Knit into front of stitch, purl into back of stitch.

Cabled Heart

Worked over 27 sts; see chart for details.

2 × 2 Ribbing

(worked in rnds over a multiple of 4 sts)

Rnd 1: *K2, p2; rep from * to end of rnd.

Rep Rnd 1 for patt.

Instructions

This shrug is knit from the top down in one piece, with raglan shaping for the sleeves. When the shrug reaches the underarms, the sleeves are joined and worked in the round. Finally, you will pick up stitches all around the garment and work the ribbing.

yoke

With straight needles, CO 35 (35, 35, 37, 37) sts.

Set-Up Row (RS): K1, kfb, k3, kfb, pm, kfb, k21 (21, 21, 23, 23), kfb, pm, kfb, k2, kfb, k2. 6 sts inc'd—41 (41, 41, 43, 43) sts.

Next Row (WS): **Purl.**

NOTE: *Move cable st markers as indicated by chart.*

Row 1 (Cable Set-Up) (RS): K1, kfb, k to last st before m, kfb, sm, kfb, place cable m, work Row 1 of Cabled Heart Chart across 23 (23, 23, 25, 25) sts, place cable m, kfb, sm, kfb, k to 3 sts from end of row, kfb, k2—8 sts inc'd (2 sts inc'd in Cabled Heart Chart). 49 (49, 49, 51, 51) sts.

NOTE: *Move cable markers out 1 st each side as indicated on chart.*

Row 2 (WS): Purl to Cabled Heart Chart, work Row 2 of Cabled Heart Chart (2 sts inc'd), purl to end of row. 51 (51, 51, 53, 53) sts.

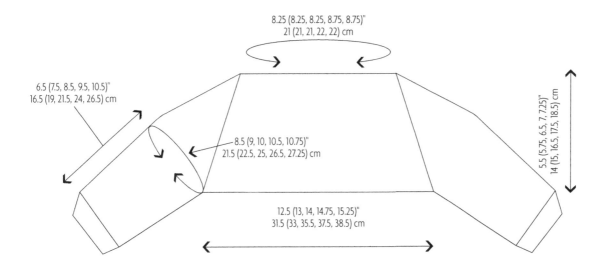

8.25 (8.25, 8.25, 8.75, 8.75)"
21 (21, 21, 22, 22) cm

6.5 (7.5, 8.5, 9.5, 10.5)"
16.5 (19, 21.5, 24, 26.5) cm

8.5 (9, 10, 10.5, 10.75)"
21.5 (22.5, 25, 26.5, 27.25) cm

5.5 (5.75, 6.5, 7, 7.25)"
14 (15, 16.5, 17.5, 18.5) cm

12.5 (13, 14, 14.75, 15.25)"
31.5 (33, 35.5, 37.5, 38.5) cm

Row 3 (RS): K1, kfb, k to last st before m, kfb, sm, kfb, sl cable m, work Row 3 of Cabled Heart Chart, sl cable m, kfb, sm, kfb, k to last 3 sts, kfb, k2—10 sts inc'd (4 incs from Cabled Heart Chart). 61 (61, 61, 63, 63) sts.

Sizes 21 (23, 25)"/53.5 (58.5, 63.5) cm only: Move cable markers out 1 st each side as indicated on chart.

Next Row (WS): Purl to Cabled Heart Chart, work Cabled Heart Chart (4 sts inc'd), purl to end of row. 65 (65, 65, 67, 67) sts.

Next Row (RS): K1, kfb, k to last st before m, kfb, sm, kfb, k to cable m, sl cable m, work Cabled Heart Chart, sl cable m, k to last st before m, kfb, sm, kfb, k to last 3 sts, kfb, k2—6 sts inc'd. 71 (71, 71, 73, 73) sts.

Continue to work in est'd patt until Cabled Heart Chart is complete—30 rows have been worked in total. 125 (125, 125, 127, 127) sts. Remove cable markers, and continue in St st.

Size 21" (53.5cm) only: Yoke is now complete.

Continue working incs as set and work 0 (2, 6, 8, 10) more rows. 125 (131, 143, 151, 157) sts.

Set sts aside; do not break yarn.

sleeves

Place first 36 (38, 42, 44, 46) sts on larger dpns, remove raglan m, and join to work in the round.

Work even in St st until sleeve measures 5 (6, 7, 8, 9)"/12.5 (15, 18, 20.5, 23) cm.

Dec Rnd: Dec 0 (2, 2, 0, 2) sts evenly over this rnd. 36 (36, 40, 44, 44) sts.

Switch to smaller dpns and work in 2 × 2 Ribbing for 1.5" (4cm).

BO all sts in patt.

Slip next 53 (55, 59, 63, 65) sts onto circular needle and hold for ribbing later.

Remove m, place final 36 (38, 42, 44, 46) sts on larger dpns and join to work in the rnd. Rejoin yarn and complete as for first sleeve.

ribbing

With RS facing, rejoin yarn and knit across the 53 (55, 59, 63, 65) sts from circular needle, pick up and knit 24 (25, 27, 30, 31) sts from bottom to top on right front, pick up and knit 35 (35, 35, 37, 37) sts from

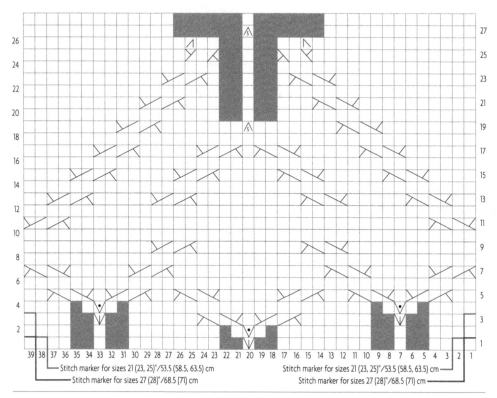

Cabled Heart Chart

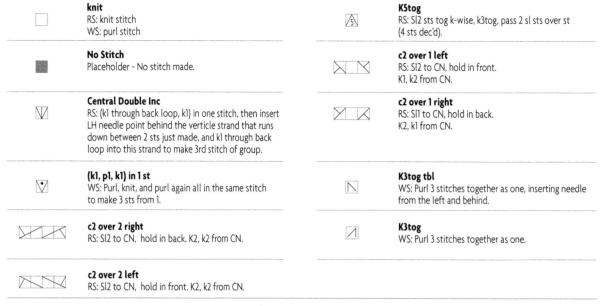

	knit		K5tog
	RS: knit stitch WS: purl stitch		RS: Sl2 sts tog k-wise, k3tog, pass 2 sl sts over st (4 sts dec'd).

knit
RS: knit stitch
WS: purl stitch

No Stitch
Placeholder - No stitch made.

Central Double Inc
RS: (k1 through back loop, k1) in one stitch, then insert LH needle point behind the verticle strand that runs down between 2 sts just made, and k1 through back loop into this strand to make 3rd stitch of group.

(k1, p1, k1) in 1 st
WS: Purl, knit, and purl again all in the same stitch to make 3 sts from 1.

c2 over 2 right
RS: Sl2 to CN, hold in back. K2, k2 from CN.

c2 over 2 left
RS: Sl2 to CN, hold in front. K2, k2 from CN.

K5tog
RS: Sl2 sts tog k-wise, k3tog, pass 2 sl sts over st (4 sts dec'd).

c2 over 1 left
RS: Sl2 to CN, hold in front. K1, k2 from CN.

c2 over 1 right
RS: Sl1 to CN, hold in back. K2, k1 from CN.

K3tog tbl
WS: Purl 3 stitches together as one, inserting needle from the left and behind.

K3tog
WS: Purl 3 stitches together as one.

Legend

CO sts at back of neck, pick up and knit 24 (25, 27, 30, 31) sts from top to bottom down left front, pm for start of rnd. 136 (140, 148, 160, 164) sts.

Pm after 51 (55, 59, 63, 63) sts, pm after 75 (79, 87, 91, 95) sts, pm after 111 (115, 119, 131, 131) sts.

Work in 2 × 2 Ribbing for 4 rnds.

Inc Rnd 1: [Work to last st before m, pfb, sm, pfb] 3 times, work to last 2 sts in rnd, pfb, pfb. 8 sts inc'd—144 (148, 156, 168, 172) sts.

Work 1 rnd in 2 × 2 Ribbing, working new sts as purl.

Inc Rnd 2: [Work to last st before m, pfkb (*see Pattern Notes*), sm, kfpb (*see Pattern Notes*)]

3 times, work to last 3 sts, pfkb, kfpb, p1—8 sts inc'd. 152 (156, 164, 176, 180) sts.

Full 2 × 2 Ribbing can now be est'd.

Continue until ribbing measures 2.5" (6.5cm).

BO all sts loosely.

Finishing

With tapestry needle, weave in all loose ends.

Block to dimensions given on schematic.

Caherciveen (Boy's Hooded Vest)

caherciveen

Boy's Hooded Vest

If you have little boys who are always warm, this hooded vest may be ideal for them. The dramatic staghorn cable is very simple to knit, but looks far more elaborate than it is! Low-key I-cord edging is used for a smooth, professional-looking finish. The subtle heathery greens in this yarn will suit any little boy's wardrobe and will go with everything.

size

To fit actual chest circumference up to: 21 (23, 25, 27, 28)"/53.5 (58.5, 63.5, 68.5, 71) cm

Suggested ages: 2 (4, 6, 8, 10) years

2–4" (5–10cm) of positive ease is recommended.

finished measurements

Chest circumference: 24.25 (27, 29, 30.75, 31.75)"/ 61.5 (68.5, 73.5, 78, 80.5) cm

Length: 14.75 (16.75, 18.25, 19.25, 20.25)"/37.5 (42.5, 46.5, 49, 51.5) cm

Size 29" (73.5cm) modeled on a 7-year-old with 2" (5cm) positive ease.

materials

- Kerry Woollen Mills "Aran Wool" (100% Wool; 350 yd./320m per 200g skein); Color: Green Bushes; 2 (2, 2, 2, 3) skeins
- US 9 (5.5mm) double-pointed needles
- US 8 (5mm) circular needle, 24" (60cm) length, *or size needed to obtain gauge*
- US 8 (5mm) straight needles
- US 7 (4.5mm) circular needle, 24" (60cm) length
- Cable needle
- Stitch markers
- Stitch holders
- Tapestry needle
- Safety pin
- 1 toggle button, 1.5" (4cm) size

gauge

17 sts × 22 rows = 4" (10cm) in St st on US 8 (5mm) needles

Staghorn Cable measures 3" (7.5cm) across

pattern notes

For m1, M1R, M1L, short-row (w&t), three-needle bind-off, and I-cord bind-off techniques, please see the "Knitting Techniques" appendix.

2 × 2 Ribbing

(worked in rnds over a multiple of 4 sts)

Rnd 1: *K2, p2; rep from * to end of rnd.

Rep Rnd 1 for patt.

Staghorn Cable

Worked over 16 sts; see chart for details.

Instructions

This vest is knit from the bottom up in the round until the armholes, then you will work the front and back separately and join at the shoulder.

body

NOTE: *When working in the rnd, all rows of the chart are read from right to left. After you divide for the armholes, you will work flat so you should read the chart from right to left on RS rows and from left to right on WS rows.*

With smaller circular needle, CO 108 (116, 124, 132, 136) sts, pm for start of rnd, join to work in the rnd taking care not to twist sts.

Work in 2 × 2 Ribbing until piece measures 2" (5cm).

With larger circular needle, knit 1 rnd and inc 12 sts evenly spaced. 120 (128, 136, 144, 148) sts.

K8 (10, 10, 12, 12) sts, work the first 8 sts of Staghorn Cable Chart, k6 (6, 8, 8, 9) sts, work all 16 sts of Staghorn Cable Chart, k6 (6, 8, 8, 9) sts, work last 8 sts of Staghorn Cable Chart (sts 9–16), k8 (10, 10, 12, 12) sts, pm for side seam, rep from * to *.

Cont in est'd patt until body measures 9 (10.5, 11.5, 12, 12.5)"/23 (26.5, 29, 30.5, 32) cm, ending with an odd rnd.

Divide for Armholes

Work in patt to 2 (3, 3, 4, 4) sts before side seam m; with straight needles, BO 4 (6, 6, 8, 8) sts, work in patt to 2 (3, 3, 4, 4) sts before end of rnd; pick up circular needle and BO 4 (6, 6, 8, 8) sts, removing beg of rnd m as you go. *Sts on straight needle will be worked later for front.* 56 (58, 62, 64, 66) sts front and back.

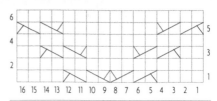

Staghorn Cable Chart

	knit RS: knit stitch WS: purl stitch
	c2 over 2 right RS: Sl2 to CN, hold in back. K2, k2 from CN.
	c2 over 2 left RS: Sl2 to CN, hold in front. K2, k2 from CN.

Legend

back

Continue on sts on circular needle for back only.

Dec Row (RS): K1, ssk, work in patt to last 3 sts, k2tog, k1. 54 (56, 60, 62, 64) sts—2 sts dec'd.

Dec Row (WS): P1, p2tog, work in patt to last 3 sts, ssp, p1. 52 (54, 58, 60, 62) sts—2 sts dec'd.

Maintaining patt, dec only on RS rows 2 more times. 48 (50, 54, 56, 58) sts.

Work in patt until armhole measures 5.5 (6, 6.5, 7, 7.5)"/14 (15, 16.5, 18, 19) cm from BO sts, ending with a WS row.

Short-row Shoulder Shaping

Rows 1 & 2: Work in patt to last 6 (6, 7, 7, 7) sts, w&t.

Rows 3 & 4: Work in patt to last 12 (12, 14, 14, 14) sts, w&t.

Work 2 more rows in patt, picking up all wraps as you pass them. Break yarn, leaving long tail.**

Place 13 (14, 15, 16, 16) sts from each end on holders for shoulders, rem 22 (22, 24, 24, 26) sts are held for back of hood. *Make note of last row of chart worked because cable continues for hood.*

FRONT

*You will divide for the neckline and **at the same time** work armhole decreases. Both sides of the front are worked at the same time with 2 balls of yarn. After the staghorn cable is split, you will work both sides of the cable independently.*

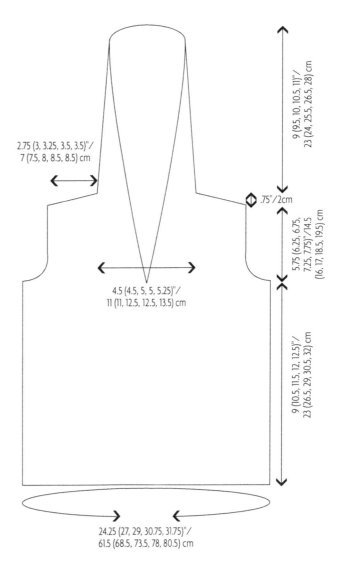

2.75 (3, 3.25, 3.5, 3.5)"/
7 (7.5, 8, 8.5, 8.5) cm

.75"/2cm

9 (9.5, 10, 10.5, 11)"/
23 (24, 25.5, 26.5, 28) cm

5.75 (6.25, 6.75, 7.25, 7.75)"/14.5 (16, 17, 18.5, 19.5) cm

4.5 (4.5, 5, 5, 5.25)"/
11 (11, 12.5, 12.5, 13.5) cm

9 (10.5, 11.5, 12, 12.5)"/
23 (26.5, 29, 30.5, 32) cm

24.25 (27, 29, 30.75, 31.75)"/
61.5 (68.5, 73.5, 78, 80.5) cm

Divide for Neck

Reattach yarn to sts held on straight needle to work front.

Dec Row (RS): K1, ssk, work in patt over 14 (15, 17, 18, 19) sts, k2tog, k1, work sts 1–8 of Staghorn Cable Chart, m1, join new ball of yarn, m1, work sts 9–16 of Staghorn Cable Chart, k1, ssk, work in patt to last 3 sts, k2tog, k1. 27 (28, 30, 31, 32) sts each side.

Dec Row (WS): P1, p2tog, work in patt to last 3 sts, ssp, p1. 26 (27, 29, 30, 31) sts each side.

Cont to work both sides in patt and dec only on RS rows 2 more times. 24 (25, 27, 28, 29) sts each side.

Work 5 more rows in patt, ending with a WS row.

Neckline Shaping

Neckline Dec Row (RS): Work in patt to last 12 sts of left front, k2tog, k1, work sts 1–8 of Staghorn Cable Chart, k1; k1, work sts 9–16 of Staghorn Cable Chart, k1, ssk, work in patt to end of row. 23 (24, 26, 27, 28) sts each side.

Work Neckline Dec Row every 10th row 1 (1, 2, 2, 2) more time(s). 22 (23, 24, 25, 26) sts each side.

Work in patt until armhole measures 5.5 (6, 6.5, 7, 7.5)"/14 (15, 16.5, 18, 19) cm from bound-off under-arm sts, ending with a WS row.

Work short-row shoulder shaping as for back from ** to ** working across right and left side of front each row.

Place 13 (14, 15, 16, 16) sts from each end on dpns for shoulder, and join to back shoulders using three-needle bind-off.

9 (9, 9, 9, 10) sts rem on each side for front of hood.

hood

With larger circular needle and working in est'd patt, work 9 (9, 9, 9, 10) sts from right front, pick up and knit 2 sts in gap, work across 22 (22, 24, 24, 26) sts held for back neck, pick up and knit 2 sts in gap and then work rem 9 (9, 9, 9, 10) sts from left front. 44 (44, 46, 46, 50) sts.

Work 1 WS row and pm at both sides of central staghorn cable for hood incs.

Inc Row (RS): Work in est'd patt to m, M1R, sm, cont to work staghorn cable, sm, M1L, work in est'd patt to end of row. 46 (46, 48, 48, 52) sts.

Work Inc Row every RS row 13 more times and then every 4th row 3 (4, 4, 5, 5) times. 78 (80, 82, 84, 88) sts. Remove inc m.

Work even in patt until hood measures 9 (9.5, 10, 10.5, 11)"/23 (24, 25.5, 26.5, 28) cm from shoulder, ending with a RS row.

Place half of the sts on each end of the circular needle, fold work so RS are touching and work three-needle bind-off using third needle.

Finishing

armholes

With smaller circular needle and RS facing, starting at center of underarm BO sts, pick up and knit 2 (3, 3, 4, 4) sts, pick up and knit 3 sts for every 4 rows around armhole to BO sts, pick up rem 2 (3, 3, 4, 4) sts from BO underarm sts, pm for start of rnd. Using dpn, work I-cord bind-off around armhole edging.

neck edging

Place safety pin on left side of neck opening to mark buttonhole position.

With smaller circular needle and RS facing, beg at the bottom on right side of neck, pick up and knit 3 sts for every 4 rows around neck opening and hood.

With dpn, work I-cord bind-off around neck opening to safety pin. Work I-cord to length desired (approx 1.5" [4cm] worked in sample) for buttonhole loop, then continue to work I-cord bind-off to end of neck.

Join ends of I-cord together.

Sew in button opposite buttonhole.

Weave in loose ends with tapestry needle.

Block sweater to dimensions given in schematic. Take care to block cables gently.

ushendale
woollen mills

Cushendale Woollen Mills is located in the little village of Graig-Na-Managh (pronounced *Greg-na-man-a*), County Kilkenny, Ireland. This picturesque village has the Barrow River running through it, giving the village a unique and distinctive character. A winding path along the river takes you past boats moored along the river wall on one side and postcard-pretty cottages and gardens on the other side. As you continue walking, it quickly changes from village to countryside.

This is the entrance to the Cushendale Woollen Mills Shop.

economically unviable to produce the yarn because the mill process requires a great deal of water.

From here I made my way to several more rooms where *carding* (combing and cleaning the wool), dyeing, drying, and weaving take place. The dyeing, washing, and drying room was steaming hot and smelled like a giant wet dog from all the wet wool. Large dye vats are dotted around the room and a giant washing machine sloshes wet yarn around in circles. And, finally, there is a huge custom-built drying room where both yarn and finished products (rugs and blankets) are hung to dry.

Cushendale uses a blend of 50 percent Irish and 50 percent New Zealand fleece. Irish wool fleece is very durable, but the softer fleece from New Zealand is blended with it to produce a hard-wearing yarn that is also soft and pleasant to wear. The mill dyes all their wool yarn before spinning it. The wool is dyed into nine different colors and then these are blended to produce

The mill felt very open and welcoming as I entered through the small shop filled with colorful knitted goods and emerged into the mill itself.

A beautiful hand-weaving loom dominates the first room behind the shop. Philip Cushen, the owner of the mill, led me into the mill itself, where the yarn is spun.

From the window of the spinning room, I could see the clear stream passing by that is an essential ingredient in the mill's success. The pure, untainted water is the original reason the mill was located here. Because the water does not have *bog taint* (brown staining of the water due to passing through the bog) or lime, it can be used untreated to wash the yarn. If the mill had to treat the water, then it would be

Cushendale's Yarn Varieties

Cushendale Woollen Mill spins a wide variety of yarns including wool, mohair, boucle mohair, and cotton chenille. Some of these yarns are currently only used for weaving, but three are available as hand-knitting yarn: "DK Wool," "Wool 4-ply/Sport," and "Mohair Boucle." The most widely available yarn they produce is their wool yarn, which is sold in a dk weight and sport weight. In recent years, Cushendale has also begun producing boucle mohair (70% mohair, 30% wool) for hand knitting. This yarn can produce a warm, soft, and beautiful fabric.

View of a cone winder at work inside the mill.

the wide variety of subtle color shades that they sell. The blending of the different colors during the spinning process gives the yarn color a depth and richness that is impossible to achieve if the yarn is dyed after spinning.

Milling has a long history in this village, from 1204 when the Cistercian monks built a monastery and mill to the mid-1600s when Flemish and Belgian weavers came to the area. Woolen manufacturing has also been in the Cushen family for many generations. In the 1800s, Patrick Cushen began woolen manufacturing and in 1925 the family bought one of the original monastery mills.

This mill is still a family-run business operated by the Cushen family. Philip Cushen is full of new ideas, pushing forward the possibilities of yarn in Ireland. He has modified the machinery and investigated new yarns and sheep breeds to ensure that his mill will continue to thrive and move forward into the twenty-first century.

NOTE: *For information on where to buy Cushendale Woollen Mills yarn, please refer to the "Yarn Availability and Substitutions" appendix.*

yarn review
Cushendale "DK Wool"

Weight: 112g (219 yd./200m)
Material: 100% wool
Needle Size: US 6–7 (4–4.5mm)
Gauge: 20–21 sts × 26–30 rows = 4" (10cm) in St st

This is a tightly spun yarn that has several layers of colors. From a distance, the yarn color appears to be solid, but on closer inspection you can see the subtle layers of complementary shades. This yarn has a firm hand while you are knitting it, which is very useful when knitting garments that need a little structure and shape. Washing this yarn does soften the fabric a little, but it is not a dramatic change.

This yarn creates a lovely texture when knit with US size 7 (4.5mm) needles, giving a relatively firm fabric but still with nice movement to it. You can also knit with a size 6 (4mm) needle if a firmer fabric is needed. This firmer fabric is useful when knitting cables that you really want to "pop."

Knockmore (Men's Twisted Stitch Sweater)

knockmore

Men's Twisted Stitch Sweater

Knitting for the man in your life is a delicate balance between an interesting knit for you and a finished piece that is simple enough that he will want to wear it. The fascinating construction method used in this sweater will keep you interested all the way to the final stitch! Knit in the round from the bottom up, the sleeves and body are joined at the yoke and the saddle-shoulder shaping is created in one piece using decreases. Details are kept simple with ribbed edging, a twisted stitch lattice border, and side panels for a streamlined fit.

size

To fit actual chest circumference up to: 34 (38, 42, 46, 50)"/86 (96.5, 106.5, 117, 127) cm.

3–5" (7.5–12.5cm) of positive ease is recommended.

finished measurements

Chest circumference: 37.5 (41.5, 45.5, 49.5, 53.5)"/95.5 (106, 116, 126, 136) cm

Length: 24.5 (26.25, 27, 28.25, 29.5)"/62 (66.5, 68.5, 72, 75) cm

Size 45.5" (116cm) modeled with 5" (12.5cm) of positive ease.

materials

- Cushendale "DK Wool" (100% wool; 219 yd./200m per 112g skein); Color: Light Orange; 5 (6, 7, 7, 8) skeins

  NOTE: *This yarn is sold in the U.S. as Black Water Abbey "2-ply Worsted."*

- US 7 (4.5mm) circular needle, 32" (80cm) length or longer, *or size needed to obtain gauge*
- US 6 (4mm) circular needle, 32" (80cm) length or longer
- US 7 (4.5mm) double-pointed needles
- US 6 (4mm) double-pointed needles
- Detachable stitch markers
- Waste yarn
- Tapestry needle

gauge

20 sts × 26 rows = 4" (10cm) in St st on larger needles

Lattice Chart

Worked over a multiple of 6 sts + 4; see chart for details.

Chart A (left-slanting cable)

Worked over 16 sts; see chart for details.

Chart B (right-slanting cable)

Worked over 16 sts; see chart for details.

Instructions

This sweater is knit in one piece from the bottom up. After the body and sleeves are completed, you will knit the yoke together in one piece.

body

With smaller circular needle, CO 180 (204, 228, 240, 264) sts, pm for start of rnd (and to also mark first side seam), pm at center of sts for other side seam, and join to work in the rnd taking care not to twist sts.

Rnd 1: *Sl 1 p-wise, work 2 × 2 Ribbing to last st before m, sl 1, sm; rep from * once.

Rnd 2: *K1, work 2 × 2 Ribbing to last st before m, k1, sm; rep from * once.

Rep these 2 rnds 2 times.

Switch to larger circular needle.

Next Rnd: *Sl 1, work Lattice Chart (red boxes indicate patt repeats) across *all* sts to last st before m, sl 1, sm; rep from * once.

NOTE: *Each side of sweater has 14 (16, 18, 19, 21) full repeats of Lattice Chart and 4 edge sts worked.*

Next Rnd: *K1, work Lattice Chart to last st before m, k1, sm; rep from * once.

Work in est'd patt until 12 rows of Lattice Chart are complete.

pattern notes

For the M1L and M1R increase techniques, please see the "Knitting Techniques" appendix.

2 × 2 Ribbing (rnds)

Rnd 1: *K2, p2; rep from * to end of rnd.

Rep Rnd 1 for patt.

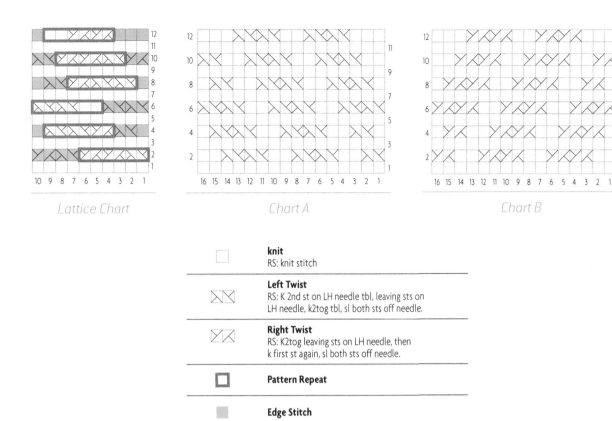

Lattice Chart   **Chart A**   **Chart B**

	knit
	RS: knit stitch

	Left Twist
	RS: K 2nd st on LH needle tbl, leaving sts on LH needle, k2tog tbl, sl both sts off needle.

	Right Twist
	RS: K2tog leaving sts on LH needle, then k first st again, sl both sts off needle.

	Pattern Repeat

	Edge Stitch

Legend

Next Rnd: Sl 1, work Chart A, p1, k to 18 sts before side m **and at the same time** inc 4 (2, 0, 4, 2) sts evenly, p1, work Chart B, sl 1, sm, sl 1, work Chart A, p1, k to last 18 sts before end of rnd **and at the same time** inc 4 (2, 0, 4, 2) sts evenly, p1, work Chart B, sl 1. 188 (208, 228, 248, 268) sts.

Continue in est'd patt (sl st before and after markers every other rnd) until body measures 16 (16.5, 17, 17.5, 18)"/40.5 (42, 43, 44.5, 45.5) cm.

BO 6 (6, 7, 8, 9) sts, work in patt to 6 (6, 7, 8, 9) sts before side m, BO 12 (12, 14, 16, 18) sts, work in patt to last 6 (6, 7, 8, 9) sts, BO 6 (6, 7, 8, 9) sts, break yarn and pull through last st. *Make note of last patt rnd worked.* 82 (92, 100, 108, 116) sts each for front and back.

Set body aside until sleeves are complete.

Right sleeve

With smaller dpns, CO 52 (52, 56, 56, 64) sts, pm for start of rnd.

Work in 2 × 2 Ribbing for 5 rnds.

Next Rnd: Work sts as they appear and, **at the same time,** inc 0 (0, 2, 2, 0) sts evenly spaced. 52 (52, 58, 58, 64) sts.

Switch to larger dpns.

Next Rnd: P1, work Chart A, p1, work Lattice Chart to end of rnd.

Work in est'd patt until Lattice Chart is complete.

Next Rnd: P1, work Chart A, p1, k17 (17, 20, 20, 23), pm for new start of rnd. 17 (17, 20, 20, 23) sts remain unworked in the rnd. Remove older marker.

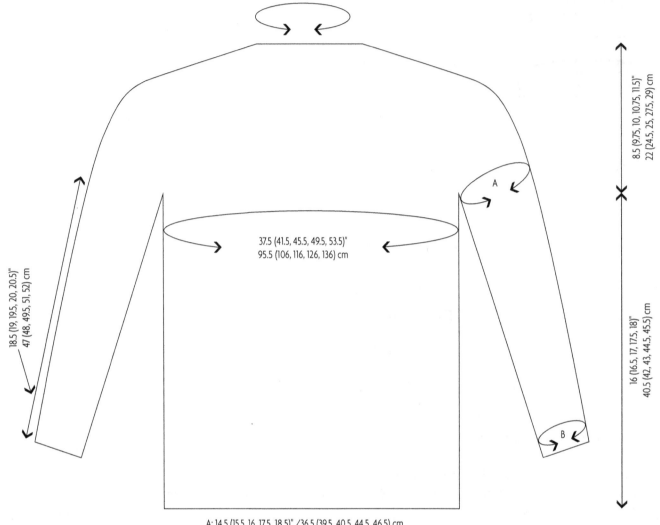

15.25 (16, 17.5, 18.5, 19.25)"
38.5 (40.5, 44.5, 46.5, 49) cm

8.5 (9.75, 10, 10.75, 11.5)"
22 (24.5, 25, 27.5, 29) cm

37.5 (41.5, 45.5, 49.5, 53.5)"
95.5 (106, 116, 126, 136) cm

18.5 (19, 19.5, 20, 20.5)"
47 (48, 49.5, 51, 52) cm

16 (16.5, 17, 17.5, 18)"
40.5 (42, 43, 44.5, 45.5) cm

A

B

A: 14.5 (15.5, 16, 17.5, 18.5)" /36.5 (39.5, 40.5, 44.5, 46.5) cm
B: 10.5 (10.5, 11.5, 11.5, 13)" /26.5 (26.5, 29.5, 29.5, 32.5) cm

Sleeve Inc Rnd: K1, M1L, work in patt to last st, M1R, k1.

Continuing in est'd patt, work Sleeve Inc Rnd every 9 (7, 9, 7, 7) rnds, 4 (6, 8, 13, 2) times, then every 10 (8, 10, 8, 8) rnds, 5 (6, 2, 1, 11) time(s). 72 (78, 80, 88, 92) sts.

Cont in patt *without* shaping until sleeve measures 18.5 (19, 19.5, 20, 20.5)"/47 (48, 49.5, 51, 52) cm. BO 6 (6, 7, 8, 9) sts, work in patt to last 6 (6, 7, 8, 9) sts, BO 6 (6, 7, 8, 9) sts, break yarn and pull through last st. 60 (66, 66, 72, 74) sts. *Make note of last patt rnd worked.*

Transfer sts to holder or waste yarn.

left sleeve

Work as for right sleeve, replacing Chart A with Chart B. Leave sts on the needles.

yoke

You will join the body and sleeves and work the yoke in one piece. Charts A and B continue on the sleeves all the way up the shoulder saddles. Maintain Charts A and B on the sides of the body as much as possible until all sts in the twist panels have been dec'd. If the 2 sts needed for a twist aren't available, work the lone st as knit instead.

Reattach yarn, work across front body sts, pm, work across right sleeve sts, pm, work across back body sts, pm, work across left sleeve sts, pm for end of rnd. 284 (316, 332, 360, 380) sts.

Cont to work in patt for 19 rnds.

Yoke Shaping

As you decrease sts, change to dpns when there are insufficient sts for circular needle.

Body Dec Rnd: Ssk, work to 2 sts before m, k2tog, work in patt across sleeve to m, sm, ssk, work in patt to 2 sts before m, k2tog, work in patt to end of rnd.

Rep Body Dec Rnd 5 (9, 10, 13, 16) more times. 260 (276, 288, 304, 312) sts.

Move each marker over 1 st into body sections so that 2 more sts are in each sleeve section and 2 fewer sts are in the front and back sections. This will keep the seam lines tidy.

Sleeve Dec Rnd: *Work in patt to m, sm, ssk, work sleeve sts to last 2 sts before m, k2tog; rep from *.

Work Sleeve Dec Rnd 20 (23, 23, 26, 27) more times. 176 (180, 192, 196, 200) sts.

Move all markers over 1 st into sleeve sections. Front and back will have 2 more sts; sleeves will have 2 fewer sts. This will maintain the seam lines.

Body Dec Rnd: Work to 2 sts before m, k2tog, work across sleeve to m, sm, ssk, work to 2 sts before m, k2tog, work to end of rnd, sm, ssk (this is at beg of next rnd).

Work this rnd 9 more times. 136 (140, 152, 156, 160) sts.

Work across front of body to right sleeve, **work 18 sleeve sts in patt, sm, ssk, turn work, sl 1 p-wise, work in patt to m, sm, p2tog, turn work.

Next Row (RS): Sl 1 k-wise, work to m, sm, ssk, turn work.

Next Row (WS): Sl 1 p-wise, work to m, sm, p2tog, turn work.

Work these 2 rows 7 more times**. 118 (122, 134, 138, 142) sts.

Work across back sts to left sleeve and rep from ** to ** for second saddle shoulder. 100 (104, 116, 120, 124) sts.

Neck Shaping

Move back markers so seam st is with sleeve sts.

Work in patt to third m (left shoulder), sm, ssk, turn work, sl 1 p-wise, p to next m, sm, p2tog, turn work.

Next Row (RS): Sl 1 k-wise, work to m, sm, ssk, turn work.

Next Row (WS): Sl 1 p-wise, work to m, sm, p2tog, turn work.

Work these 2 rows 7 more times. 82 (86, 98, 102, 106) sts.

Finishing

neckband

Change to smaller dpns.

Knit 1 rnd and dec 6 (6, 10, 10, 10) sts evenly spaced. 76 (80, 88, 92, 96) sts.

Work in 2 × 2 Ribbing for 5 rnds.

BO all sts in patt.

Sew underarm seams.

Weave in loose ends.

Block sweater to dimensions given on schematic.

Saddle Shoulders

NOTE: *Charts A and B are being worked flat in this section. Read all RS rows (even rows) from right to left and WS rows (odd rows) from left to right.*

ballyrasset

Twisted Stitch Hat

Hats make perfect gifts because they are fast to knit and very usable. The subtle twisted stitch pattern worked on this hat is enjoyable to knit and creates a hat that is wearable and cozy. The stitch pattern is simple and attractive, and creates a truly unisex pattern. The warmth of the Cushendale wool will keep you snug all through the winter and the wide variety of colors to choose from makes it easy to find the perfect color.

size

To fit actual head circumference up to: 22 (24)"/ 56 (61) cm

2–2.5" (5–6.5cm) of negative ease is recommended to ensure a snug fit.

finished measurements

Circumference: 20 (22.25)"/51 (56.5) cm

Shown in 20" (51cm) size modeled with 2" (5cm) of negative ease.

materials

- Cushendale "DK Wool" (100% wool; 219 yd./200m per 112g skein); color: Light Orange; 1 (1) skein

  NOTE: *This yarn is sold in the U.S. as Black Water Abbey "2-ply Worsted."*
- US 7 (4.5mm) circular needle, 16" (40cm) length, *or size needed to obtain gauge*
- US 6 (4mm) circular needle, 16" (40cm) length
- US 7 (4.5mm) double-pointed needles
- Stitch markers
- Waste yarn
- Tapestry needle

gauge

20 sts × 26 rows = 4" (10cm) in St st on larger needle

23 sts × 26 rows = 4" (10cm) in Lattice Chart patt on larger needle

pattern notes

Lattice Chart

(worked over a multiple of 6 sts + 4)

See Lattice Chart and legend in the "Knockmore: Men's Twisted Stitch Sweater" pattern on p. 47.

NOTE: *Red boxes on chart indicate patt repeats.*

Small Hat Chart

Worked over 54 sts; see chart for details.

Large Hat Chart

Worked over 60 sts; see chart for details.

2 × 2 Ribbing (rnds)

(worked over a multiple of 4 sts)

Rnd 1: K2, p2; rep to end of rnd.

Rep Rnd 1 for patt.

Instructions

With smaller circular needle, CO 108 (120) sts. Join to work in the rnd taking care not to twist sts, and pm for start of rnd.

Work in 2 × 2 Ribbing for 4 rnds.

Change to larger circular needle.

Rnd 1: Work 52 (58) sts from Lattice Chart beg with Rnd 1, sl 2 sts p-wise wyib, work 52 (58) sts from Lattice Chart, sl 2 sts p-wise wyib.

Rnd 2: Work 52 (58) sts from Lattice Chart, k2, work 52 (58) sts from Lattice Chart, k2.

Cont working in est'd patt until 12 rnds of Lattice Chart are complete.

Next Rnd: Begin Hat Chart for your size. Work the 54 (60) sts of Rnd 1 of Small Hat (Large Hat) Chart twice to complete the rnd.

Continue through Rnd 12 of Hat Chart, then work Rnds 1–12 once more.

NOTE: Work Rnds 1–12 an additional time if a longer hat is desired.

CROWN Shaping

Work Rnds 13–33 (13–35) of Small Hat (Large Hat) Chart, changing to dpns when necessary. 26 (32) sts.

Next Rnd: K2tog 13 (16) times. 13 (16) sts.

Next Rnd: K2tog 6 (8) times, k1 (0). 7 (8) sts.

Break yarn. Thread tapestry needle with tail and pull through remaining sts. Pull to close top and fasten.

Finishing

Weave in any loose ends. Block to dimensions given. (It may be helpful to use a curved bowl for blocking to hold the shape of the hat.)

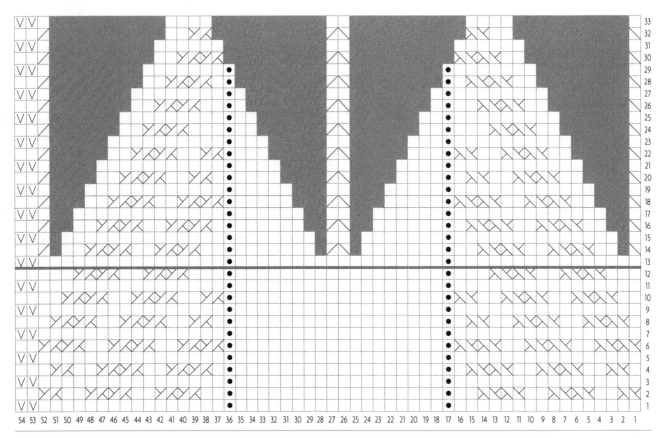

Small Hat Chart

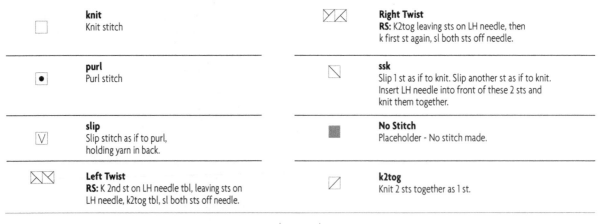

	knit		Right Twist
	Knit stitch		**RS:** K2tog leaving sts on LH needle, then k first st again, sl both sts off needle.

	purl		ssk
	Purl stitch		Slip 1 st as if to knit. Slip another st as if to knit. Insert LH needle into front of these 2 sts and knit them together.

	slip		No Stitch
	Slip stitch as if to purl, holding yarn in back.		Placeholder - No stitch made.

	Left Twist		k2tog
	RS: K 2nd st on LH needle tbl, leaving sts on LH needle, k2tog tbl, sl both sts off needle.		Knit 2 sts together as 1 st.

Legend

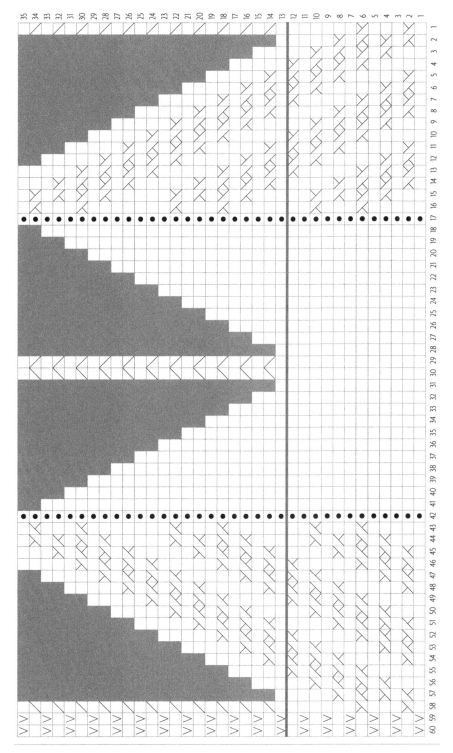

Large Hat Chart

Dangan (Cable-and-Lace Square Blanket/Shawl)

danʃan

Cable-and-Lace Square Blanket/Shawl

Delicate and warm, this lightweight blanket will keep your knees warm on cool evenings or would also make a beautiful baby blanket. This piece is elegant and light enough to work wonderfully as a shawl, too. The larger size is big enough to fold over and use as a gernerously sized shawl, while the smaller size will keep your shoulders warm. It is knit at a loose gauge with 4-ply (sport weight) yarn, which creates a light and open blanket after blocking.

Finished measurements

29 (47)"/74 (120) cm square after blocking

Shown in smaller size.

materials

- Cushendale "4-ply/Sport" (100% wool; 368 yd./336m per 112g skein); Color: Autumn; 2 (5) skeins

  NOTE: *This yarn is sold in the U.S. as Black Water Abbey "2-ply Sport Weight."*

- US 7 (4.5mm) double-pointed needles, *or size needed to obtain gauge*
- US 7 (4.5mm) circular needle, 32" (80cm) length
- Stitch markers
- Cable needle
- Tapestry needle

gauge

18 sts × 23 rows = 4" (10cm) in St st, blocked

16 sts × 20 rows = 4" (10cm) in Feather-and-Fan Lace Patt, blocked

pattern notes

For elastic bind-off instructions, please see the "Knitting Techniques" appendix.

Feather-and-Fan Lace

(worked in rnds over a multiple of 18 sts)

Also shown in chart form at center of Lace Increase Chart in red box.

Rnd 1: *(K2tog) 3 times, (yo, k1) 6 times, (k2tog) 3 times; rep from * to end.

Rnd 2: Purl.

Rnds 3 & 4: Knit.

C6B (6-st Cable)
(worked in the rnd over 6 sts)

Rnd 1: Sl 3 sts onto CN and hold to back of work, k3, k3 from cable needle.

Rnds 2–6: Knit.

Lace Increase Pattern
Worked over 18 sts at beginning of chart, 54 sts when chart complete; see chart for details.

Instructions
You will start this blanket/shawl at the center with only 4 stitches and work outwards. You will increase

on each side of four cables to create square shaping. The blanket ends with a generous Feather-and-Fan lace edging.

CENTER
With dpns, CO 4 sts. Place 1 st on each needle, pm for start of rnd, and join to work in the rnd.

Next Rnd: Kfb 4 times. 8 sts.

Next Rnd: Kfb 8 times. 16 sts.

Next Rnd: Kfb 16 times. 32 sts.

Set-up Rnd: (K6, pm, yo, k2, yo, pm) 4 times, (last marker already in place)—8 sts inc'd. 40 sts.

Rnd 1: (C6B, sm, k to next m, sm) 4 times.

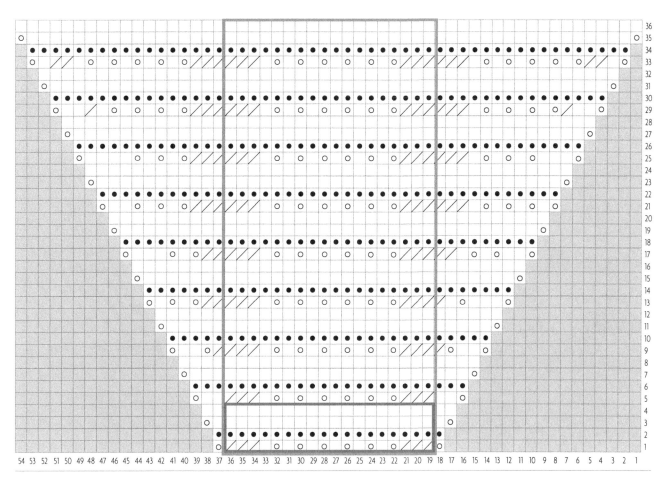

Lace Increase Chart

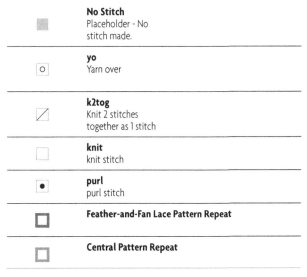

	No Stitch Placeholder - No stitch made.
○	**yo** Yarn over
╱	**k2tog** Knit 2 stitches together as 1 stitch
	knit knit stitch
•	**purl** purl stitch
☐	**Feather-and-Fan Lace Pattern Repeat**
☐	**Central Pattern Repeat**

Legend

Rnd 2: (C6B, sm, yo, k to next m, yo, sm) 4 times—8 sts inc'd. 48 sts.

Rep these 2 rnds, turning cable every 6th round, until there are 240 (384) sts total, with 54 (90) sts between each cable.

Knit 1 rnd.

lace edging

Continue with C6B cables as set and beg working Lace Increase Chart between cables; green central box repeated 3 (5) times each side. Work Rnds 1–36 once (twice), then Rnds 1–12 once. You will add repeats of the green boxed Feather-and-Fan Lace Pattern each side every time you rep Rnd 1. 432 (720) sts.

You will have 6 edge sts on each side of cable, giving you 18 sts to work the Feather-and-Fan Lace Pattern at the edge.

NOTE: *If you wish to work a larger blanket, then work 1 more rep of the Lace Increase Chart ending on rnd 12. Ensure that you increase yarn requirements if you choose to work a larger blanket.*

edging

You are no longer working incs, all sts are now worked in Feather-and-Fan Lace Pattern.

Next Rnd: Knit 12 sts, pm for new end of rnd, remove previous end of rnd marker.

Work in Feather-and-Fan Lace Pattern until 4 rnds are complete.

BO all sts using the elastic bind-off.

Finishing

Block finished piece, stretching to open up the lace.

Weave in loose ends.

Belville (Women's Tweed Yoke Sweater)

belville

Women's Tweed Yoke Sweater

This simple yet elegant sweater is a perfect blend of yarn and pattern. The gently speckled color variations in the yarn blend together to form a subtle combination for the tweed-pattern yoke. Knit in the round from the bottom up, folded hems at the bottom and sleeve cuffs provide a finished look. At the yoke, you will join the sleeves and body together and work in the round.

This sweater looks great when worn with just a T-shirt underneath or with a matching collared shirt. Experiment to find your own style.

size

To fit actual bust circumference up to: 27 (31, 35, 39, 43, 47, 51)"/68.5 (78.5, 89, 99, 109, 119.5, 129.5) cm

1" (2.5cm) of positive ease is recommended.

finished measurements

Chest circumference: 28 (32, 36, 40, 44, 48, 52)"/71 (81.5, 91.5, 101.5, 112, 122, 132) cm

Length: 22 (22.5, 23, 23.5, 24, 24.5, 25)"/56 (57, 58.5, 59.5, 61, 62, 63.5) cm

Size 36" (91.5cm) modeled with 1" (2.5cm) of positive ease.

materials

- Cushendale "DK Wool" (100% wool; 219 yd./200m per 112g skein); MC: Pink Heather, 3 (3, 3, 4, 4, 4, 5) skeins; CC: Gentian Purple, 1 skein for all sizes

  NOTE: This yarn is sold in the U.S. as Black Water Abbey "2-ply Worsted."

- US 7 (4.5mm) circular needle, 24" (60cm) length or longer, *or size needed to obtain gauge*
- US 6 (4mm) circular needle, 24"(60cm) length or longer
- US 7 (4.5mm) double-pointed needles
- US 6 (4mm) double-pointed needles
- Stitch markers, 2 of one sort, 4 contrasting
- Waste yarn
- Tapestry needle

gauge

20 sts × 26 rows = 4" (10cm) in St st on larger needles

21 sts × 32 rows = 4" (10cm) in Tweed Stitch on larger needles

pattern notes

For provisional cast-on, M1R, M1L, short rows (w&t), whipstitch, and grafting techniques, please see the "Knitting Techniques" appendix.

Tweed Stitch

(worked in rnds over a multiple of 4 sts)

Rnd 1: With CC, * Sl second st on LH needle over first st (p-wise) and onto RH needle, k3; rep from * to end of rnd.

Rnd 2: With CC, *Sl 1 st p-wise, k3; rep from * to end of rnd.

Rnd 3: With MC, K2, *sl second st on LH needle over first st (p-wise) and onto RH needle, k3; rep from * to last 2 sts, sl second st on LH needle over first st and onto RH needle, k1.

NOTE: *When working Rnd 3, the st that was slipped on the previous rnd is mounted backwards. Take care to knit into the **front** of this stitch to twist it.*

Rnd 4: With MC, knit.

Instructions

You will work the body and sleeves in the round from the bottom up. At the yoke, you will join the sleeves to the body and work them together in the round.

body
Knitted Hem

With smaller circular needle, CO 140 (160, 180, 200, 220, 240, 260) sts using provisional cast-on and waste yarn.

With CC, k70 (80, 90, 100, 110, 120, 130), pm for side seam, k to end, pm for start of rnd, join to work in rnd taking care not to twist sts.

Knit 7 more rnds.

Change to larger circular needle and purl 1 rnd.

Break CC, join MC and knit 7 rnds.

Undo provisional cast-on, placing all "live" sts on smaller circular needle.

Fold along purl ridge and hold smaller needle inside work.

*Insert larger needle into first st on front needle then first st on back needle and knit these 2 sts tog to join; rep from * to end of rnd to form knitted hem.

Knit 10 (8, 6, 6, 6, 6, 8) rnds even.

Waist Shaping

Place contrasting markers for shaping darts 17 (20, 22, 25, 27, 30, 32) sts before and after each side marker.

Waist Dec Rnd: *Work to 2 sts before first front dart m, k2tog, sm, work to second dart marker, sm, ssk; rep from * once, k to end of rnd.

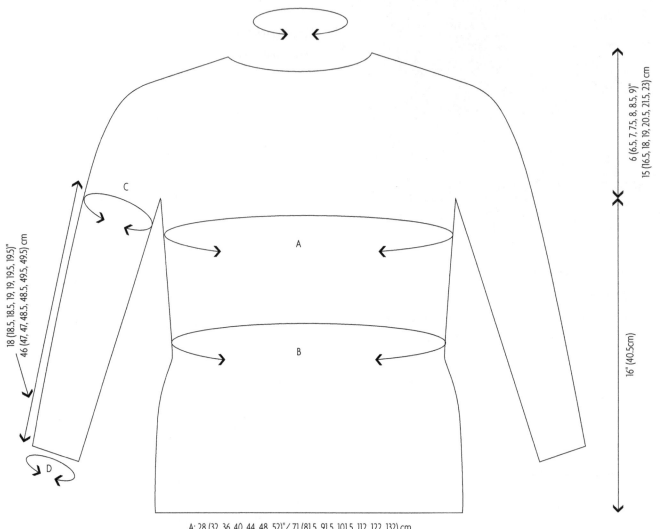

20 (22, 24, 25, 26, 27, 28)"
51 (56, 61, 63.5, 66, 68.5, 71) cm
circumference

6 (6.5, 7, 7.5, 8, 8.5, 9)"
15 (16.5, 18, 19, 20.5, 21.5, 23) cm

18 (18.5, 18.5, 19, 19, 19.5, 19.5)"
46 (47, 47, 48.5, 48.5, 49.5, 49.5) cm

16" (40.5cm)

C

A

B

D

A: 28 (32, 36, 40, 44, 48, 52)"/ 71 (81.5, 91.5, 101.5, 112, 122, 132) cm
B: 24 (28, 32, 36, 40, 44, 48)"/ 61 (71, 81.5, 91.5, 101.5, 112, 122) cm

C: 10.5 (11.25, 12, 13.25, 14.5, 16, 16.5)"/ 26.5 (28.5, 30.5, 33.5, 36.5, 40.5, 41.5) cm
D: 8.5 (8.75, 9.25, 9.5, 9.5, 10, 10.5)"/ 21.5 (22, 23.5, 24, 24, 25.5, 26.5) cm

Work Waist Dec Rnd every 5 rnds 2 more times, then every 6 rnds 2 times—20 sts dec'd. 120 (140, 160, 180, 200, 220, 240) sts.

Work 12 rnds even.

Bust Shaping

Bust Inc Rnd: * Work to first front dart m, M1R, sm, work to second dart marker, sm, M1L; rep from * once, k to end of rnd.

Work Bust Inc Rnd every 9 (10, 10, 10, 10, 10, 9) rnds 2 (4, 4, 2, 4, 4, 4) times, then every 10 (0, 0, 11, 0, 0, 0) rnds 2 (0, 0, 2, 0, 0, 0) times—20 sts inc'd. 140 (160, 180, 200, 220, 240, 260) sts.

Remove dart markers and work in St st without shaping until body measures 16" (40.5 cm).

Divide for Armholes

Work to 5 (6, 7, 8, 9, 9, 10) sts after side m, place 10 (12, 14, 16, 18, 18, 20) sts *just worked* on waste yarn (underarm for right sleeve), k to 5 (6, 7, 8, 9, 9, 10) sts past end of rnd m, place 10 (12, 14, 16, 18, 18, 20) sts *just worked* on waste yarn (underarm for left sleeve). 60 (68, 76, 84, 92, 102, 110) sts for front and back side.

Set body aside to be worked later. Do not break yarn.

sleeves

With smaller dpns, CO 42 (44, 46, 48, 48, 50, 52) sts using provisional cast-on and waste yarn.

With CC knit all sts, join to work in the rnd, pm for start of rnd.

Knit 7 rnds.

Using larger dpns, purl 1 rnd.

Break CC, join MC and knit 7 rnds.

Undo provisional cast-on, placing all "live" sts on smaller circ needle.

Fold along purl ridge and hold circ needle inside work.

*Insert larger needle into first st on front needle then first st on back needle, knit these 2 sts tog to join; rep from * to end of rnd to form knitted hem.

Work in St st until sleeve measures 2.5" (6.5 cm) from edge of folded hem.

Sleeve Inc Rnd: K1, M1L, k to last st, M1R, k1.

Work Sleeve Inc Rnd every 20 (17, 14, 12, 9, 7, 7) rnds 3 (4, 1, 8, 11, 10, 10) time(s), then every 21 (18, 15,

0, 0, 8, 8) rnds 1 (1, 5, 0, 0, 4, 4) time(s)—10 (12, 14, 18, 24, 30, 30) sts inc'd. 52 (56, 60, 66, 72, 80, 82) sts.

Work even until sleeve measures 18 (18.5, 18.5, 19, 19, 19.5, 19.5)"/46 (47, 47, 48.5, 48.5, 49.5, 49.5) cm.

Work to 5 (6, 7, 8, 9, 9, 10) sts past end of rnd, place 10 (12, 14, 16, 18, 18, 20) sts *just worked* on waste yarn and break yarn leaving long tail for grafting. 42 (44, 46, 50, 54, 62, 62) sts.

Rep for second sleeve.

yoke

Return to sts held for body. With attached yarn, knit across front, knit right sleeve sts, pm for short rows, knit back sts, pm for new start of rnd, knit left sleeve sts. 204 (224, 244, 268, 292, 328, 344) sts.

Work even in St st until yoke measures 1.5 (2, 2.5, 3, 3.5, 4, 4.5)"/4 (5, 6.5, 7.5, 9, 10, 11.5) cm.

Short-row Back Shaping

Next Row (RS): Knit to 3 sts before end of rnd m, w&t.

Next Row (WS): Purl to 3 sts before m, w&t.

Next Row (RS): Knit to 1 st before m, w&t.

Next Row (WS): Purl to 1 st before m, w&t.

Remove short-row m (between right sleeve and back); keep end of rnd m in place.

Knit to end of rnd, knitting wraps together with sts as you pass them.

Knit to last 30 (34, 38, 42, 46, 51, 55) st, place new end of rnd m.

Change to shorter needle or dpns when necessary as you shape the yoke.

Dec Rnd 1:* [K4, k2tog] 10 (14, 4, 20, 22, 14, 12) times and then [k5 (5, 5, 5, 5, 3, 3), k2tog] 6 (4, 14, 2, 2, 16, 20) times; rep from * once—32 (36, 36, 44, 48, 60, 64) sts dec'd. 172 (188, 208, 224, 244, 268, 280) sts.

Knit 1 rnd.

Work Rnds 1–4 of Tweed Stitch twice (8 rnds total).

Knit 2 rnds.

Dec Rnd 2: *[K3, k2tog] 10 (14, 4, 20, 22, 14, 12) times and then [k4 (4, 4, 4, 4, 2, 2), k2tog] 6 (4, 14, 2, 2, 16, 20) times; rep from * once—32 (36, 36, 44, 48, 60, 64) sts dec'd. 140 (152, 172, 180, 196, 208, 216) sts.

Knit 1 rnd.

Work Rnds 1–4 of Tweed Stitch twice.

Knit 2 rnds.

Dec Rnd 3: *[K3 (3, 2, 2, 1, 1, 1), k2tog] 14 (8, 14, 10, 6, 16, 12) times and then [K – (4, 3, 3, 2, 2, 2), k2tog] – (6, 6, 10, 20, 14, 18) times; rep from * once—28 (28, 40, 40, 52, 60, 60) sts dec'd. 112 (124, 132, 140, 144, 148, 156) sts.

Knit 1 rnd.

Work Rnds 1–4 of Tweed Stitch twice.

Work in St st until yoke measures 6 (6.5, 7, 7.5, 8, 8.5, 9)"/15 (16.5, 18, 19, 20.5, 21.5, 23) cm from underarm.

Short-row Neck Shaping

Next Row (RS): Knit to end of rnd, w&t.

Next Row (WS): Purl 38 (42, 44, 46, 48, 50, 52) sts, w&t.

Next Row (RS): Work to 2 sts past previous turn, w&t.

Next Row (WS): Work to 2 sts past previous turn, w&t.

Knit to end of rnd.

Dec Rnd 4: With CC, [k7 (6, 9, 7, 8, 9, 7), k2tog] 8 (2, 12, 10, 10, 8, 4) times and then [k8 (7, 0, 8, 9, 10, 8), k2tog] 4 (12, 0, 5, 4, 5, 12) times—12 (14, 12, 15, 14, 13, 16) sts dec'd. 100 (110, 120, 125, 130, 135, 140) sts.

Purl 1 rnd.

With smaller needle, knit 8 rnds.

Break yarn, leaving very long tail.

Fold seam along purl fold line and whipstitch live sts to inside of neck to form hem.

Finishing

Graft underarm sts together.

Weave in loose ends with tapestry needle.

Block to dimensions given on schematic.

ballinagree

Boy's Sweater

The geometric cable pattern on this boy's sweater is bold and masculine, creating a sweater that boys both young and old will be eager to wear. The crossed central cables are reminiscent of crossed swords on shields for your little medieval knight. In this sweater, the yarn is worked at a tighter gauge than normal which creates a more dramatic texture and makes the cables stand out from the purled background.

Worked in one piece from the bottom up in the round, you can adjust both body and sleeve lengths as you knit for the perfect fit. A simple placket and collar finish the sweater with minimal fuss. If you prefer a fold-over collar, knit until desired length to comfortably fold.

size

To fit actual chest circumference up to: 20 (23, 25, 27, 28)"/53.5 (58.5, 63.5, 68.5, 71) cm

Suggested ages: 2 (4, 6, 8, 10) years

2–4" (5–10cm) of positive ease is recommended.

finished measurements

Chest: 22.25 (25.25, 27.5, 30, 31.5)"/56.5 (64, 70, 76, 80) cm

Length: 14.5 (15.75, 16.75, 17.75, 18.75)"/36.5 (40, 42.5, 45, 48) cm

Size 25.25" (64cm) modeled on a 4-year-old with 2" (5cm) positive ease.

materials

- Cushendale "DK Wool" (100% wool; 219 yd./200m per 112g skein); Color: Sky Blue; 2 (3, 3, 4, 4) skeins

  NOTE: This yarn is sold in the U.S. as Black Water Abbey "2-ply Worsted."

- US 6 (4mm) circular needle, 24" (60cm) length, *or size needed to obtain gauge*
- US 6 (4mm) double-pointed needles
- Cable needle
- Stitch markers
- Waste yarn
- Tapestry needle

gauge

21 sts × 30 rows = 4" (10cm) in St st

26 sts × 30 rows = 4" (10cm) in 1 × 1 Ribbing

Crossed Cable Chart measures 10" (25.5cm) across

pattern notes

For pfb and grafting instructions, please see the "Knitting Techniques" appendix.

1 × 1 Ribbing (rnds and rows)

(worked over a multiple of 2 sts)

Row/Rnd 1: *K1, p1; rep from * to end of row.

Rep Row/Rnd 1 for patt.

Crossed Cable Chart

Worked over 64 sts; see chart for details.

Instructions

Knit from the bottom up in the round, the body and sleeves are joined together at the yoke which has raglan shoulder shaping.

body

With circular needle, CO 140 (156, 168, 180, 188) sts, pm for start of rnd, join to work in the rnd taking care not to twist sts.

Work in 1 × 1 Ribbing until piece measures 1.5" (4cm).

Next Rnd: P3 (7, 10, 13, 15) sts, work 64 sts of Crossed Cable Chart, p3 (7, 10, 13, 15) sts, pm for side seam, p3 (7, 10, 13, 15) sts, work 64 sts of Crossed Cable Chart, p3 (7, 10, 13, 15) sts.

Cont in est'd patt until body measures 9.5 (10, 10.25, 11, 11.75)"/24 (25.5, 26, 28, 30) cm ending with an even rnd.

Divide for Sleeve Underarms

Work in patt to 1 (1, 1, 2, 2) st(s) past side seam m, place previous 2 (2, 2, 4, 4) sts on waste yarn, work in patt to 1 (1, 1, 2, 2) st(s) past end of rnd, place previous 2 (2, 2, 4, 4) sts on waste yarn.

Do not break yarn, set body aside to be worked later. 68 (76, 82, 86, 90) sts front and back. Make note of last round worked.

Right sleeve

With dpns, CO 38 (40, 42, 44, 46) sts, pm for start of rnd, join to work in the rnd taking care not to twist sts.

Work in 1 × 1 Ribbing until sleeve measures 1.5" (4cm).

P15 (16, 17, 18, 19) sts, work first 8 sts of Crossed Cable Chart, p15 (16, 17, 18, 19) sts to end of rnd.

Work 1 rnd in patt.

Inc Rnd: P1, pfb, work in patt to last 2 sts, pfb, p1. 2 sts inc'd.

Work Inc Rnd every 15 (13, 12, 11, 12) rnds 1 (5, 4, 3, 7) time(s) and then every 16 (–, 13, 12, –) rnds 2 (–, 2, 4, –) times—8 (12, 14, 16, 16) sts inc'd. 46 (52, 56, 60, 62) sts.

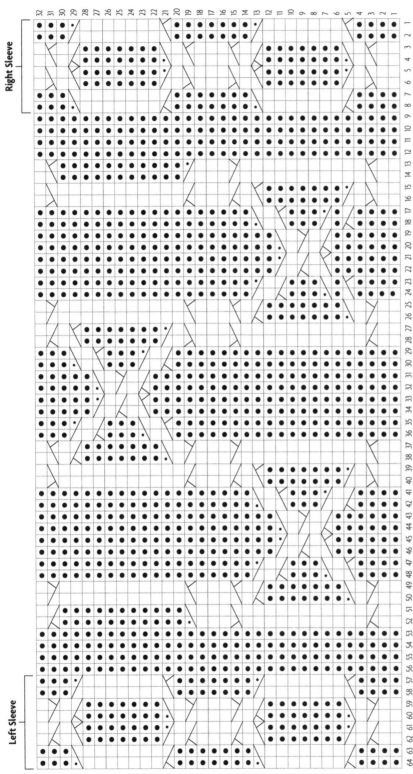

Crossed Cable Chart

purl
RS: purl stitch
WS: knit stitch

knit
RS: knit stitch
WS: purl stitch

c2 over 2 right
RS: Sl2 to CN, hold in back.
K2, k2 from CN.

c2 over 2 left
RS: Sl2 to CN, hold in front.
K2, k2 from CN.

c2 over 2 right P
RS: Sl2 to CN, hold in back.
K2, p2 from CN.

c2 over 2 left P
RS: Sl2 to CN, hold in front.
P2, k2 from CN.

Legend

Work in est'd patt until sleeve measures 10 (12, 13, 14, 15)"/ 25.5 (30.5, 33, 35.5, 38) cm ending with an odd rnd.

Divide for Sleeve Underarm

Work 1 (1, 1, 2, 2) st(s), place previous 2 (2, 2, 4, 4) sts on waste yarn.

Break yarn, leaving long tail for grafting, and set sleeve sts aside on waste yarn. 44 (50, 54, 56, 58) sts. Make note of last cable round worked.

left sleeve

Work as for left sleeve but replace first 8 sts of Crossed Cable Chart with *last* 8 sts of Crossed Cable Chart. End with same cable rnd as right sleeve.

yoke

Raglan shoulder decreases are worked every other rnd. Work each cable until there are insufficient sts to complete it, then work these sts in knit or purl to match pattern. Two sts on each side of raglan are always knit to create a smooth raglan seam.

Make sure you work Dec Rnd on odd rnd (RS) from Crossed Cable Chart so that you will work the correct rnd when dividing for the placket.

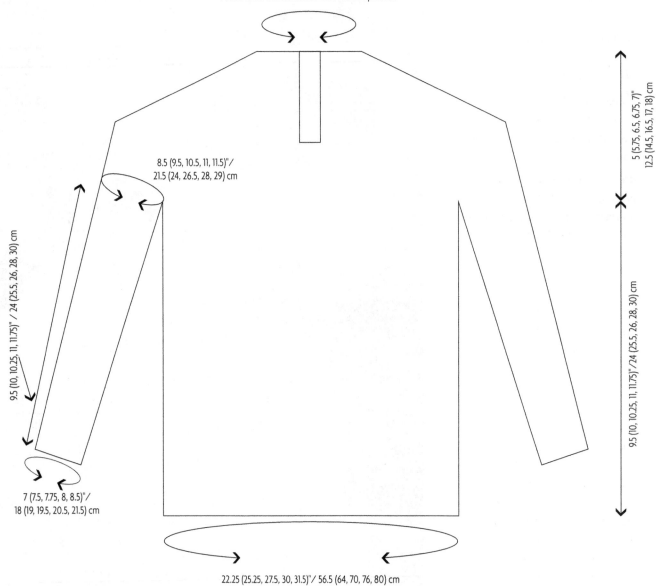

11.5 (12, 12.5, 13.25, 14)" / 29 (30.5, 32, 33.5, 35.5) cm
NOTE: Neck dimensions do NOT include placket.

8.5 (9.5, 10.5, 11, 11.5)"/
21.5 (24, 26.5, 28, 29) cm

5 (5.75, 6.5, 6.75, 7)"
12.5 (14.5, 16.5, 17, 18) cm

9.5 (10, 10.25, 11, 11.75)" / 24 (25.5, 26, 28, 30) cm

9.5 (10, 10.25, 11, 11.75)"/24 (25.5, 26, 28, 30) cm

7 (7.5, 7.75, 8, 8.5)"/
18 (19, 19.5, 20.5, 21.5) cm

22.25 (25.25, 27.5, 30, 31.5)"/ 56.5 (64, 70, 76, 80) cm

Joining Body and Sleeves

Return to sts held for body. Pm for start of rnd and first raglan, and, using yarn still attached to body, k2, work across front in patt to last 2 sts, k2, pm for raglan, k2, work across sts held for right sleeve in patt to last 2 sts, k2, pm for raglan, k2, work back of body in patt to last 2 sts, k2, pm for raglan, k2, work across sts held for left sleeve in patt to last 2 sts, k2. 224 (252, 272, 284, 296) sts.

Dec Rnd: Ssk, (work to 2 sts before m, k2tog, sm, ssk) 3 times, work to 2 sts before m, k2tog. 8 sts dec'd.

Next Rnd: Work in est'd patt, knitting 2 sts before and after each marker.

Rep these 2 rnds 10 (11, 12, 12, 12) times. 136 (156, 168, 180, 192) sts.

Divide for Neck

The center 6 sts of the Crossed Cable Chart will be bound off for the neck placket and you will continue working back and forth on the remaining sts. Be sure to divide neck on an odd-numbered row of the chart.

Dividing Rnd: Ssk, work 18 (21, 23, 25, 27) sts, BO 6 sts, (work to 2 sts before m, k2tog, sm, ssk) 3 times, work to 2 sts before m, k2tog, continue to bound-off neck sts in patt (new end of row)—14 sts dec'd. 122 (142, 154, 166, 178).

Turn work.

Next Row (WS): Work in patt to end of row.

Dec Row (RS): (Work in patt to 2 sts before m, k2tog, sm, ssk) 4 times, work in patt to end of row. 8 sts dec'd.

Rep these 2 rows 5 (7, 8, 9, 10) times, then work 1 more WS row. 74 (78, 82, 86, 90) sts.

Work in 1 × 1 Ribbing for 1" (2.5cm).

BO all sts in patt.

Finishing

FRONT bands

Right Placket

On right front neck placket, with RS facing and circular needle, beg at bottom of placket, pick up and knit 18 (22, 24, 26, 28) sts. Work in 1 × 1 Ribbing for 8 rows, or until band fits placket opening, ending with a WS row.

BO all sts in patt.

Left Placket

On left front neck placket, with RS facing and circular needle, beg at top of placket, pick up and knit 18 (22, 24, 26, 28) sts. Work as for right band.

Graft underarm seams together.

Sew bottom edges of front plackets in place.

Weave in ends with a tapestry needle.

Block sweater to dimensions given in schematic. Take care to block cables gently.

kilmanagh

Felted Tweed Handbag

The tradition of tweed woven fabrics is very strong in Ireland. The heathered yarn creates a subtle color interplay in the delicate tweed fabric. You can create your own unique and beautiful bag that uses a tweed stitch to add texture and a blending of the colors between two yarns. This bag is knit a little larger than normal and then lightly *felted* (washed to shrink) to create structure while still retaining stitch definition. You can choose between either a small handbag size or a larger tote size.

sizes

Finished Sizes (after felting):
Handbag (tote) height: 7.5 (12)"/19 (30.5) cm

Width at base: 12 (14)"/30.5 (35.5) cm

Depth at top: 4 (4.75)"/10 (12) cm

Pre-felting Sizes:
Handbag (tote) height: 8.75 (14)"/22 (35.5) cm

Width at base: 13.5 (16)"/34.5 (40.5) cm

Depth at top: 4 (4.75)"/10 (12) cm

Shown in handbag size.

materials

- Cushendale "DK Wool" (100% wool; 219 yd./200m per 112g skein); MC: dark green (Emerald); 1 (2) skein(s); CC: light green (Jade); 1 (1) skein

  NOTE: *This yarn is sold in the U.S. as Black Water Abbey "2-ply Worsted."*

- US 8 (5mm) straight needles, *or size needed to obtain gauge*
- US 8 (5mm) double-pointed needles (for I-cord bind-off)
- US 8 (5mm) circular needles, 2 sets (any length, for picking up side stitches)
- Tapestry needle
- Decorative button, 1" (2.5cm)
- Leather handle, 18" (45.5cm) long

gauge

Before Felting:
16 sts × 30 rows = 4" (10cm) in garter st

17 sts × 23 rows = 4" (10cm) in St st

21 sts × 32 rows = 4" (10cm) in Star Tweed Pattern

After Felting:
18 sts × 34 rows = 4" (10cm) in garter st

18 sts × 27 rows = 4" (10cm) in St st

21 sts × 36 rows = 4" (10cm) in Star Tweed Pattern

pattern notes
For m1 and applied I-cord instructions, please see the "Knitting Techniques" appendix.

Using dpn, CO 3 sts, slip them to the front circular needle with working yarn at right.

Using dpn, *K2, sl 1, insert needle into first st on front needle then first st on back needle and knit these 2 sts tog, pass slipped st over the st just made, sl 3 sts from dpn to circular needle, and rep from * until all picked up sts have been worked. 3 sts rem on needle.

I-cord (for button loop)
*K3, sl 3 sts from dpn back to circular needle, rep from * until desired length has been worked.

Star Tweed Pattern
(worked over a multiple of 4 sts + 1, using 2 colors: MC and CC)

Row 1 (RS): With CC, K1, *sl 1 wyib, m1, sl 1 wyib, k1, pass first sl st over next 3 sts, k1*, rep from * to * until all sts have been worked.

Row 2 (WS): With CC, Purl.

Row 3 (RS): With MC, K3, rep from * to * (on Row 1) until 2 sts remain, k2.

Row 4 (WS): With MC, purl.

Instructions
You will begin knitting this bag at the right side, knit across the base and then up the left side. Then you will pick up and knit the front and back sections.

Right side
With straight needles and MC, CO 21 (26) sts.

Work 4 rows in garter st, ending with a WS row.

Join CC and work in Star Tweed Pattern for 64 (104) rows.

Break CC.

Three-needle I-cord Bind-off
With RS facing, use a circular needle to pick up sts from right to left along the first edge you want to join. Rep with a separate circular needle on the second side.

When all sts are picked up, hold both pieces with WS together and slide sts on both needles to right end to begin work.

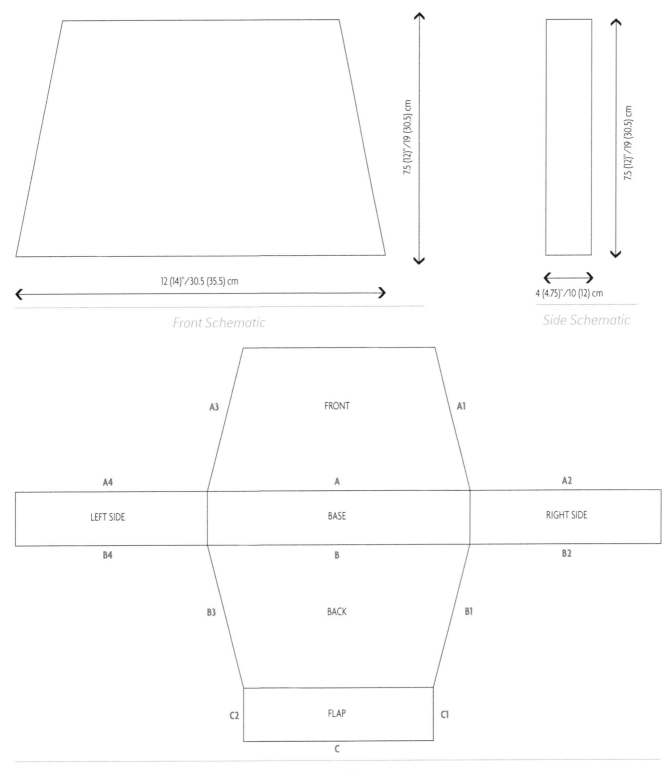

Front Schematic

7.5 (12)"/19 (30.5) cm

12 (14)"/30.5 (35.5) cm

Side Schematic

7.5 (12)"/19 (30.5) cm

4 (4.75)"/10 (12) cm

A3   FRONT   A1

A4   A   A2

LEFT SIDE   BASE   RIGHT SIDE

B4   B   B2

B3   BACK   B1

C2   FLAP   C1

C

Assembly Schematic

base

The base of the bag is worked only in MC.

Dec Row (RS): Working in garter st, dec 3 (5) sts evenly across row. 18 (21) sts.

Work in garter st for 100 (118) more rows.

Inc Row (WS): Working in garter st, inc 3 (5) sts evenly across row. 21 (26) sts.

left side

Join CC and work in Star Tweed Pattern for 64 (104) rows.

Break CC. With MC, work 4 rows in garter st.

BO all sts in patt.

FRONT

With RS facing and working from right to left, with MC pick up and knit 56 (64) sts evenly spaced along garter st bag base (side A on the assembly schematic).

**Work in St st for 7 (9) rows.

Dec Row (RS): K1, ssk, k to last 3 sts, k2tog, k1. 54 (62) sts.

Rep these 8 (10) rows 4 (6) more times. 46 (50) sts.**

Work 6 more rows in St st.

Work 4 rows in garter st.

BO all sts in patt.

back

With RS facing and working from right to left, with MC pick up and knit 56 (64) sts evenly spaced along garter st bag base (side B on the assembly schematic).

Work as for front from ** to **.

Work 10 rows in St st, ending with a RS row.

Next Row (WS): Knit to last 2 sts, k2tog. 45 (49) sts.

Join CC and work in Star Tweed Pattern for 52 (60) rows.

Break both yarns. Leave sts on straight needle to work I-cord bind-off and buttonhole later.

Finishing

See assembly schematic for numbering of sides. Bag is shown flat with inside facing up.

JOINING FRONT OF the bag

NOTES:

1. Do not BO final sts for I-cord until the seam is complete for each side.

2. When you reach a corner, work 1 row of I-cord without attaching to bag to create curve.

3. All joining is worked using MC .

With RS facing and using circular needle, pick up 33 (53) sts from right to left on side A1. Rep with second circular needle for side A2. Join sides A1 and A2 using three-needle I-cord bind-off, 3 sts rem on dpn when complete.

With circular needle, pick up 56 (64) sts across seam A, and work applied I-cord across all sts using sts from dpn; 3 sts rem on dpn when complete.

With circular needle, pick up 33 (53) sts from right to left on side A3. Rep with second circular needle for side A4. Join sides A3 and A4 using three-needle I-cord bind-off. BO final 3 I-cord sts when complete.

JOINING back OF the bag

NOTE: You will use MC when working all joins of the back of the bag.

With RS facing, pick up 56 (64) sts along seam B, work applied I-cord across all sts; 3 sts rem on dpn when complete.

With RS facing, using circular needle, pick up 33 (53) sts from right to left along side B1. Rep with second circular needle for side B2. Join sides B1 and B2 using three-needle I-cord bind-off; 3 sts rem on dpn when complete.

With circular needle, pick up 25 (30) sts along side C1, work applied I-cord across all sts using sts from dpn; 3 sts rem on dpn when complete.

Using sts on straight needle for side C, work applied I-cord across 22 (24) sts, work I-cord for 2" (5cm) (*this standard I-cord will form loop for buttonhole*), then continue applied I-cord across rem sts on straight needle; 3 sts remain on dpn when complete.

With circular needle, pick up 25 (30) sts across side C2, work applied I-cord across all sts using sts from dpn; 3 sts rem on dpn when complete.

With circular needle, pick up 33 (53) sts from right to left on side B3. Rep with second circular needle for side B4. Join sides B3 and B4 using three-needle I-cord bind-off. BO final 3 I-cord sts when complete.

Weave in all ends.

Felting the bag

Felt bag by placing in washing machine and using warm water. Check frequently and remove when it has been lightly felted.

*NOTE: Make sure you do **not** leave the bag in the machine too long; you should still be able to see individual stitches after light felting.*

Shape bag to dimensions on schematics and allow to dry. It may be necessary to insert cardboard inside the bag to shape it correctly while drying. Fold top of sides together neatly and hold in place with safety pins while drying.

Attaching the handle

Folding sides of bag to form neat fold (in same position as it was dried in), attach handle according to manufacturer's recommendations.

donegal yarns

(formerly Kilcarra Woollen Mills)

onegal is an extraordinary part of Ireland. Its sober bogs, rolling sand dunes, and steep cliffs and crags create a feeling of great mystery. It is also a land of sheep. My four-year-old son put it best during our visit when he pointed out the car window and said, "You can see the sheep in the clouds!"

I looked, and he was quite right; the mist had covered the mountainside and you could see sheep-shaped clouds floating by.

A pair of goats hanging out in front of a Donegal home.

For several days before visiting the Donegal Yarns mill, my family stayed in a small cottage at the top of Glengesh Pass. It was like we were a world away from home. While the weather in the rest of Ireland was warm and sunny the day we travelled, our time in the pass was misty and cool. It was also solitary. The cottage had no phone or Internet connection, our cell phones had no reception, and even the car radio struggled to find a signal.

But what we lacked in connectivity, we more than made up for in sheep. Sheep were everywhere! They grazed in our cottage garden, paced us when we walked along the paths, and jumped unexpectedly from the roadside ditches as we drove by. Most impressively, sheep even seemed to be suspended in midair alongside an almost vertical cliff running down to a stunning beach that we enjoyed during a short break in the mist.

Yarn and spinning have a long history in Donegal. In the 1800s, yarn was processed in homes where it was spun and dyed by hand. Although this yarn was primarily for local personal use, it was sometimes exported as well. The unique and recognizable look of modern Donegal yarn—the multicolored flecks, called "nepps," that are dotted throughout the yarn—may have originated in this home-spinning industry. The

different fleece colors sometimes got mixed up in the carding process, creating the original "tweed effect." This tweed effect is still a signature aspect of Donegal yarns, but now it does not happen by accident (see sidebar).

The Donegal Yarns mill is a much larger operation than the other mills in Ireland. The mill, located in the village of Kilcar, is busy and buzzing with activity. Unlike the other mills I visited, they do not have a factory shop attached directly to it. However, just down the road in the village, the Studio Donegal shop sells a good selection of their yarn, as well as knitted and woven goods made from yarn spun at the Donegal Yarns mill.

The history of the mill stretches back over a century. In the late 1890s, the Congested Districts Board centralized the distribution and marketing of textile goods in Donegal. In the late 1920s, after the creation of the Irish Free State government, their responsibilities were handed over to Gaeltarra Eireann, which was a semi-state body (a partially state-owned enterprise). Under this body, the textile industry was built up over the following 50 years until it was the largest employer in southwest Donegal.

In the 1970s, this body was separated into three divisions: weaving, knitwear, and spinning. The spinning division moved to Kilcar and was known as Gaeltarra Yarns. They supplied all the local knitwear producers and started to build an international recognition of the Donegal tweed-effect yarn.

The mill has experienced two further name changes. In the 1980s, it was renamed Kilcarra Yarns, and in June 2008, it was renamed Donegal Yarns in order to reflect the international nature of the company and to signify the importance of its Donegal heritage and its signature tweed-effect yarns. Due to these name changes, you can still find Donegal Yarns under several different labels; some yarns still have the

Dyeing vats inside the Donegal Yarns mill.

The Recipe for Tweed

While the original Donegal tweed may have emerged by accident, it is now a carefully designed effect, following specific "recipes" to blend a variety of different colored and textured fleeces.

Despite the availability of local sheep, the fleece for Donegal Yarns comes from abroad, usually New Zealand, Australia, and Norway. Irish sheep are bred for their meat, so the fleece produced is often coarse and in poor condition. The internationally sourced fleeces are blended to create a perfect mixture of fiber length, softness, and good *handle* (the way a yarn feels to the touch). The multicolored "nepps" (flecks of yarn) are created from 100 percent wool before the yarn is spun. They are then added to the fleece and blended together. Following different recipes, the various fleeces and nepps are mechanically blended with oil (to reduce static) in a blending chamber (picture a room-size tumble drier) and then baled. This blending process unifies the different fleece colors and ensures that the colored nepps are well distributed throughout the yarn. This process also helps to create a more uniform yarn structure.

Donegal Yarns has created a unique process to keep the nepps intact when the yarn is spun (rather than being blended in with the rest of the yarn) so they hold their shape and unique color. Donegal's "Aran Tweed" yarn is very lightly spun to create a hand-spun effect, and the long fiber length makes the yarn more stable. The finished yarn consists of a base color mixture of up to six individual colors with up to another seven or eight contrasting solid flecks (nepps) dotted along the surface of the yarn.

"Kilcarra" label or even their Irish distributor's label, "Studio Donegal."

The final name change happened a couple of years after the company changed status from a semi-state body to a privately owned company. The company is now owned by four directors who have hired a managing director, Chris Weiniger, to oversee the operation of the mill. Chris, who guided me through the mill's operations, has tremendous enthusiasm for yarn and in particular for Donegal yarn. When he started working at the mill, 60 percent of their yarn

Dyed fleece waiting to be spun.

yarn review

Donegal Yarns "Aran Tweed"

Weight: 50g (88 yd./80m)
Material: 100% wool
Needle Size: US 7–8 (4.5–5mm)
Gauge: 17–18 sts × 24 rows = 4" (10cm) in St st

This is a loosely spun, colourful yarn; the nepps (flecks) of different color are scattered throughout which makes for colorful knitting. This means that even when you are knitting just plain stockinette your knitting has color and textural interest. There is a homespun quality to this yarn due to variations in the thickness (thick-and-thin effect) although these aren't extreme. This yarn changes *dramatically* with washing; it blooms and softens up considerably creating a wonderful fabric. I highly recommend that you wash your swatch before you knit a complete garment to see the difference.

Due to the loosely spun nature of this yarn, you can comfortably knit it using a variety of needle sizes. US size 7 (4.5mm) or 8 (5mm) needles provide the nicest texture and the gauge ranges from 17–18 stitches per 4" (10cm).

was produced for the domestic market. Within 12 months, they reversed it so that 60 percent of their yarn was exported. This shift in the business plan was critical in order for Donegal Yarns to thrive in such a small country; with such a small domestic population, Irish companies need to export products if they are to grow in a sustainable way.

Although the tweed-effect yarn is the signature yarn produced in Donegal, they also produce several other yarns (see www.donegalyarns.com for the full

range). The *"Irish Heather"* range of yarns, for example, is an Aran-weight yarn that is produced without the tweed flecks and is suitable for all hand knitting. The *"Soft Donegal"* range is produced using merino wool and it has the signature tweed effect as well as having more of a twist to the yarn than Donegal Yarns classic *"Aran Tweed."* As well as producing yarns under their own label (distributed in Ireland by Studio Donegal), Donegal Yarns produce yarns for several other yarn lines (for example, Debbie Bliss "Donegal Luxury Tweed Aran" and MaggiKnits "Irish Tweed"), so keep an eye out for their signature flecks!

NOTE: *For more information on where to buy Donegal Yarns, please refer to the "Yarn Availability and Substitutions" appendix.*

Killybegs (Women's Honeycomb Cardigan)

killybegs

Women's Honeycomb Cardigan

The traditional honeycomb cable stitch has long been associated with the Aran Islands off the western coast of Ireland. In a traditional pattern, this stitch is often used as an all-over accent panel. However, the honeycomb stitch has never been used like it is here in this cabled cardigan! The cable panel extends at the waist to create a naturally slim waist and decreases are worked around the yoke for a flattering and unique garment. Worked in a subtle tweed green, the soft texture of the yarn creates an undulating texture with the cables.

size

To fit actual bust circumference up to: 28 (32, 36, 40, 44, 48, 52)"/71 (81.5, 91.5, 101.5, 112, 122, 132) cm

0–2" (0–5cm) of positive ease is recommended.

finished measurements

Bust circumference: 28.5 (32, 36, 40.5, 44.5, 48.5, 52.5)"/72.5 (81.5, 91.5, 103, 113, 123, 133.5) cm

Length: 23.25 (23.5, 24, 24.5, 25, 25.5, 25.75)"/59 (59.5, 61, 62, 63.5, 65, 65.5) cm

Size 36" (91.5cm) modeled with 1" (2.5cm) positive ease.

materials

- Donegal Yarns "Aran Tweed" (100% wool; 88 yd./80m per 50g skein); Color: Green (4824); 10 (11, 12, 13, 14, 15, 16) skeins

  NOTE: *This yarn is also sold under the "Kilcarra" and "Studio Donegal" labels.*

- US 8 (5mm) circular needle, 32" (80cm) length (or longer for larger sizes), *or size needed to obtain gauge*

- US 7 (4.5mm) circular needle, 32" (80cm) length (or longer for larger sizes)

- US 8 (5mm) double-pointed needles

- Cable needle

- Removable stitch markers

- Waste yarn

- Tapestry needle

- 9–13 hook and eye closures

gauge

18 sts × 24 rows = 4" in St st on larger needle

24 sts × 26 rows = 4" over Chart A on larger needle

pattern notes

For I-cord cast-on, M1R, M1L, short rows (w&t), I-cord bind-off, and applied I-cord techniques, please see the "Knitting Techniques" appendix.

Next Row (RS): K12 (14, 17, 18, 21, 24, 27), pm, work Chart A over 8 sts, pm, k24 (28, 32, 38, 42, 46, 50), pm, work Chart A over 8 sts, pm, k24 (28, 32, 38, 42, 46, 50), pm, work Chart A over 8 sts, pm, k24 (28, 32, 38, 42, 46, 50), pm, work Chart A over 8 sts, pm, k12 (14, 17, 18, 21, 24, 27).

Next Row (WS): P12 (14, 17, 18, 21, 24, 27), work Chart A between m, p24 (28, 32, 38, 42, 46, 50), work Chart A between m, p24 (28, 32, 38, 42, 46, 50), work Chart A between m, p24 (28, 32, 38, 42, 46, 50), work Chart A between m, p12 (14, 17, 18, 21, 24, 27).

Continue working in est'd patt until Chart A has been worked 5 times.

Chart A
Worked over 8 sts; see chart for details.

Chart B
Worked over 24 sts; see chart for details.

Chart C
Worked over 16 sts; see chart for details.

Instructions

You will knit the body of this cardigan flat in one piece from the bottom up. The sleeves are knit in the round, starting at the cuff. At the yoke, you will join the body and sleeves together and knit flat in one piece.

body

Using larger circular needle, CO 128 (144, 162, 182, 200, 218, 236) sts using I-cord cast-on.

Next Row (WS): Purl.

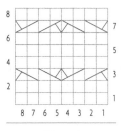

Chart A

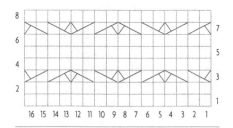

Chart C

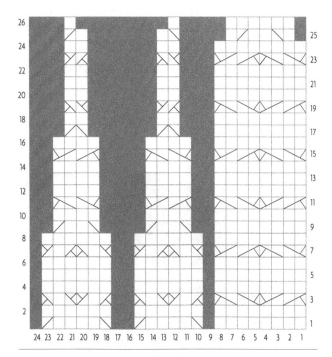

Chart B

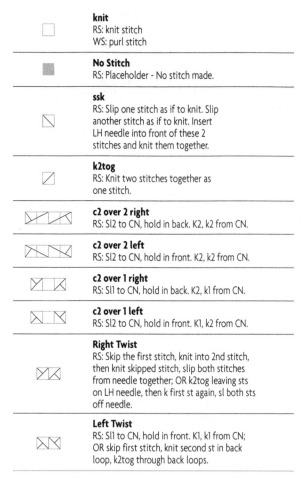

	knit
	RS: knit stitch
	WS: purl stitch

	No Stitch
	RS: Placeholder - No stitch made.

	ssk
	RS: Slip one stitch as if to knit. Slip another stitch as if to knit. Insert LH needle into front of these 2 stitches and knit them together.

	k2tog
	RS: Knit two stitches together as one stitch.

	c2 over 2 right
	RS: Sl2 to CN, hold in back. K2, k2 from CN.

	c2 over 2 left
	RS: Sl2 to CN, hold in front. K2, k2 from CN.

	c2 over 1 right
	RS: Sl1 to CN, hold in back. K2, k1 from CN.

	c2 over 1 left
	RS: Sl2 to CN, hold in front. K1, k2 from CN.

	Right Twist
	RS: Skip the first stitch, knit into 2nd stitch, then knit skipped stitch, slip both stitches from needle together; OR k2tog leaving sts on LH needle, then k first st again, sl both sts off needle.

	Left Twist
	RS: Sl1 to CN, hold in front. K1, k1 from CN; OR skip first stitch, knit second st in back loop, k2tog through back loops.

Legend

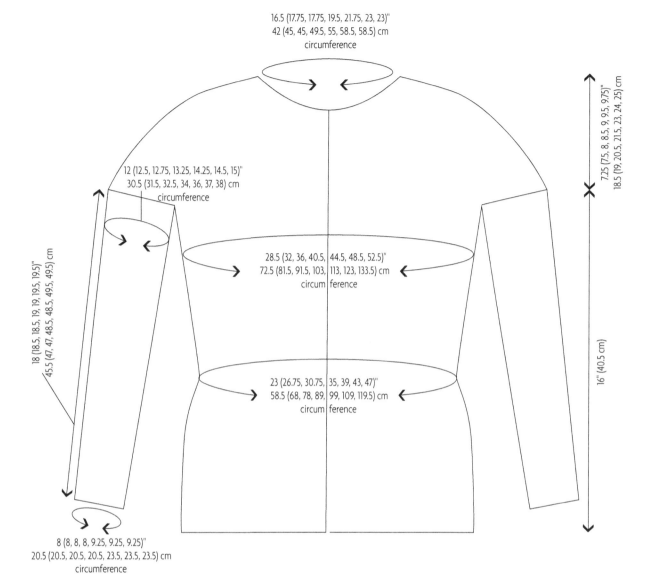

16.5 (17.75, 17.75, 19.5, 21.75, 23, 23)"
42 (45, 45, 49.5, 55, 58.5, 58.5) cm
circumference

7.25 (7.5, 8, 8.5, 9, 9.5, 9.75)"
18.5 (19, 20.5, 21.5, 23, 24, 25) cm

12 (12.5, 12.75, 13.25, 14.25, 14.5, 15)"
30.5 (31.5, 32.5, 34, 36, 37, 38) cm
circumference

28.5 (32, 36, 40.5, 44.5, 48.5, 52.5)"
72.5 (81.5, 91.5, 103, 113, 123, 133.5) cm
circumference

18 (18.5, 18.5, 19, 19, 19.5, 19.5)"
45.5 (47, 47, 48.5, 48.5, 49.5, 49.5) cm

23 (26.75, 30.75, 35, 39, 43, 47)"
58.5 (68, 78, 89, 99, 109, 119.5) cm
circumference

16" (40.5 cm)

8 (8, 8, 8, 9.25, 9.25, 9.25)"
20.5 (20.5, 20.5, 20.5, 23.5, 23.5, 23.5) cm
circumference

Waist Shaping

Move markers out 4 sts on *each* side of pattern panels so there are 16 sts between each set of markers. Begin working Chart C between markers. Continue working in est'd patt until Chart C has been worked once.

Move markers out 4 sts on each side of pattern panels so there are 24 sts between each set of markers.

Work the 8-st rep of Chart A 3 times between each set of markers.

Continue to work in est'd patt until 2 reps of Chart A have been worked.

Switch to smaller circular needle. Move markers in 4 sts on each side of pattern panels so there are 16 sts between each set of markers. Work Chart C between markers. Continue working in est'd patt until Chart C has been worked once.

Switch to larger circular needle. Move markers in 4 sts on each side of pattern panels so there are 8 sts between markers. Work Chart A between markers. Continue working in est'd patt until Chart A has been worked once.

Remove markers and work in St st until piece measures 16" (40.5cm) or desired length to underarm, ending with a RS row.

Next Row (WS): P28 (32, 34, 39, 43, 48, 50), BO 8 (8, 13, 13, 14, 13, 18) sts, p56 (64, 68, 78, 86, 96, 100), BO 8 (8, 13, 13, 14, 13, 18) sts, p to end of row and set aside. Do *not* break yarn. 112 (128, 136, 156, 172, 192, 200) sts.

sleeves

With dpns, CO 48 (48, 48, 48, 56, 56, 56) sts using I-cord cast-on, join to work in the rnd and pm to indicate start of rnd.

Begin working Chart A in the round across all sts.

NOTE: Because you are now working in the rnd, read all chart rows from right to left.

Work through 8 rows of Chart A twice.

Next Rnd: K16, pm, work 16 (16, 16, 16, 24, 24, 24) sts in Chart A, pm, k16.

Continue in est'd patt through Row 8 of Chart A.

Move markers in 4 (4, 4, 4, 8, 8, 8) sts each side.

NOTE: For the first 4 sizes, use only the first 8 sts of Chart C over the next 8 rnds.

Continue to work 8 sts between markers following Chart C (C, C, C, A, A, A) for 8 rnds. Remove markers.

Inc Rnd: K1, M1R, k to last st, M1L, k1. 50 (50, 50, 50, 58, 58, 58) sts.

Knit 25 (19, 15, 13, 20, 16, 13) rnds.

Rep these 26 (20, 16, 14, 21, 17, 14) rnds 2 (3, 4, 5, 3, 4, 5) more times. 54 (56, 58, 60, 64, 66, 68) sts.

Work without shaping until sleeve measures 18 (18.5, 18.5, 19, 19, 19.5, 19.5)"/45.5 (47, 47, 48.5, 48.5, 49.5, 49.5) cm in length.

BO 4 (4, 6, 6, 7, 6, 9) sts, k to last 4 (4, 7, 7, 7, 7, 9) sts, and BO rem sts. Cut yarn and pull through last st to secure. 46 (48, 45, 47, 50, 53, 50) sts.

Place sleeve sts on waste yarn to hold for yoke.

Make second sleeve the same way.

yoke

Return to sts held on circular needle for body; yarn is attached, ready to work a RS row.

Next Row (RS): With circular needle, k28 (32, 34, 39, 43, 48, 50) from right front of cardigan, k46 (48, 45, 47, 50, 53, 50) sleeve sts, k56 (64, 68, 78, 86, 96, 100) from back of cardigan, k46 (48, 45, 47, 50, 53, 50) sleeve sts, k28 (32, 34, 39, 43, 48, 50) from left front of cardigan. 204 (224, 226, 250, 272, 298, 300) sts.

Next Row (WS): Purl. **Sizes 28 and 52 only:** Dec 1 st at start and end of row. **Sizes 32 and 44 only:** M1 at start and end of row. 202 (226, 226, 250, 274, 298, 298) sts.

Work in St st for 2 (4, 0, 2, 6, 8, 10) rows.

Chart Set-up Row (RS): K1, *work Chart A over next 8 sts, pm, k16, pm; rep from * to last 9 sts, work 8 sts in Chart A, k1.

Cont in est'd patt until Chart A has been worked 1 (1, 2, 2, 2, 2, 2) time(s).

Next Row (RS): K1, follow Chart A to last st, k1.

Cont in est'd patt until Chart A is completed once.

NOTE: You will now decrease within the pattern following Chart B.

Yoke Dec Row (RS): K1, *work Chart B; rep from * to last m, work Chart A, k1.

Work in est'd patt until 24 rows of Chart B are completed.

Row 25 (RS): Work from Chart B to last m, sm, ssk, k4, k2tog, k1. 72 (80, 80, 88, 96, 104, 104) sts.

Row 26 (WS): Purl.

Change to smaller circular needle.

Short-row Neck Shaping

Please see the "Knitting Techniques" appendix for specific instructions on working short rows (w&t).

Row 1 (RS): K54 (60, 60, 66, 72, 78, 78), w&t.

Row 2 (WS): P36 (40, 40, 44, 48, 52, 52) w&t.

Row 3 (RS): K34 (38, 38, 42, 46, 50, 50) w&t.

Row 4 (WS): P32 (36, 36, 40, 44, 48, 48) w&t.

Work in St st for 2 rows, taking care to pick up and knit all wraps together with the sts they wrap as you encounter them.

With larger circular needle, BO using I-cord bind-off.

Finishing

Sew the bound-off sts from sleeve and body together at underarm.

Starting at the bottom right front, work applied I-cord up the right front of the cardigan.

Starting at top of left front, work applied I-cord down left front of cardigan.

Sew together the ends of the applied I-cord and the I-cord bind-off at the neck.

Attach hook and eye closures to the front bands of the cardigan evenly spaced. Ensure you attach enough closures so that the edges of the cardigan stay smoothly together. (On the sample, the hook and eye closure spacing is approx 2"/5 cm.)

Weave in loose ends with a tapestry needle.

Block sweater to dimensions given on schematic.

Bundoran (Women's Honeycomb Beret)

bundoran

Women's Honeycomb Beret

The great thing about berets is that they never go out of style and are versatile to wear. Wear this stylish beret to the side, pulled down over your ears for warmth, or sitting on the back of your head. This beret's all-over honeycomb cable creates visual interest while still being subtle enough not to dominate the hat.

When knitting a hat, the finished measurement of the band should be approximately 2" (5cm) less than your actual head measurement to ensure that it will stay in place and provide a snug fit.

size

To fit actual head circumference: 20–22 (23–24)"/51–56 (58.5–61) cm

Approximately 2–3" (5–8 cm) of negative ease is recommended.

finished measurements

Band circumference: 17.75 (19.5)"/45 (49.5) cm

Shown in small, slouchy version.

materials

- Donegal Yarns "Aran Tweed" (100% wool; 88 yd./80m per 50g skein); Color: Green (4824); 2 (3) skeins, standard version; 2 (3) skeins, slouchy version

  NOTE: This yarn is also sold under the "Kilcarra" and "Studio Donegal" labels.

- US 8 (5mm) circular needle, 16" (40cm) length, *or size needed to obtain gauge*
- US 7 (4.5mm) circular needle, 16" (40cm) length, *or size needed to obtain gauge*
- US 8 (5mm) double-pointed needles
- Cable needle
- Stitch markers
- Tapestry needle

gauge

18 sts × 24 rows = 4" (10cm) in St st on larger needles

18 sts × 26 rows = 4" (10cm) in 1 × 1 Ribbing on smaller needles, lightly stretched

pattern notes

For m1 and cdd techniques, please see the "Knitting Techniques" appendix.

1 × 1 Ribbing (rnds)

(worked in rnds over an even number of sts)

Rnd 1: *K1, p1, rep from * to end of rnd.

Rep Rnd 1 for pattern.

Honeycomb Pattern

Worked over 16 sts; see chart for details.

Instructions

Knit from the bottom up, in the round, choose the beret style that best suits you.

With smaller circular needle, CO 80 (88) sts, pm for start of rnd and join to work in the rnd, being careful not to twist sts.

Work in St st for 6 rnds, then work in 1 × 1 Ribbing for 6 rnds. Follow directions for the standard or slouchy beret, below, according to your preference.

standard beret

Inc Rnd: [K2, m1] 16 (32) times, then [k3, m1] 16 (8) times. 112 (128) sts.

Switch to larger circular needle.

Beg with Rnd 1, *work 16 sts of Honeycomb Chart, pm, rep from * around. There are 7 (8) markers.

Work Rnds 1–8 from chart twice.

Work rnds 9–37 from chart. 7 (8) sts.

NOTE: *When there are too few sts for circular needle, switch to dpns.*

slouchy beret

Refer to the "Knitting Techniques" appendix for cdd (centered double decrease) instructions.

Inc Rnd: [K1, m1] 48 (24) times and then [k2, m1] 16 (32) times. 144 (144) sts.

Switch to larger circular needle.

Beg with Rnd 1, *work 16 sts of Honeycomb Chart, pm, rep from * around. There are 9 markers.

Work rnds 1–8 from chart twice.

Work rnds 9–16 from chart twice.

Work rnds 17–37 from chart. 9 (9) sts.

Cdd 3 times. 3 (3) sts.

NOTE: *When there are too few sts for circular needle, switch to dpns.*

Finishing

Break yarn. With tapestry needle, thread yarn through rem sts and weave in snugly.

Using a plate or a circle of cardboard, block hat to desired size.

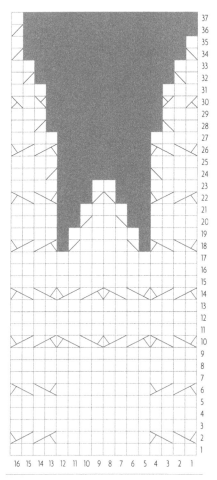

Honeycomb Chart

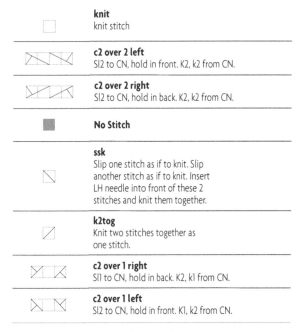

	knit
	knit stitch
	c2 over 2 left
	Sl2 to CN, hold in front. K2, k2 from CN.
	c2 over 2 right
	Sl2 to CN, hold in back. K2, k2 from CN.
	No Stitch
	ssk
	Slip one stitch as if to knit. Slip another stitch as if to knit. Insert LH needle into front of these 2 stitches and knit them together.
	k2tog
	Knit two stitches together as one stitch.
	c2 over 1 right
	Sl1 to CN, hold in back. K2, k1 from CN.
	c2 over 1 left
	Sl2 to CN, hold in front. K1, k2 from CN.

Legend

ardara

Women's Tunic Cardigan

Leggings and snug-fitting jeans are very flattering when worn with longer, tunic-length cardigans and tops. Long lines make this hip-length tunic flattering to wear. The cable repeat running up its length accentuates this effect.

Knit from the bottom up in one piece, sleeves are cast on as you reach them; you'll work the edging after the body is finished. Waist shaping is worked along the faux seam lines at the sides and is emphasized by the knitted belt. Instructions are provided for buttonholes; however, if you wish to fasten this tunic with just the belt, then work both front bands without buttonholes.

size

To fit actual bust circumference up to: 29.25 (32.75, 36.75, 40.5, 45.25, 48.75, 52.75)"/74.5 (83.5, 93.5, 103, 115, 124, 134) cm

1–3" (2.5–7.5 cm) of positive ease is recommended.

finished measurements

Bust circumference (with buttonband closed): 30.25 (33.75, 37.75, 41.5, 46.25, 49.75, 53.75)"/ 77 (86, 96, 105.5, 117.5, 126.5, 136.5) cm

Length: 28.5 (29.25, 30, 30.75, 30.75, 31, 31.25)"/ 72.5 (74.5, 76, 78, 78, 78.5, 79.5) cm

Size 37.75" (96 cm) modeled with 2.5" (6.5 cm) of positive ease.

materials

- Donegal Yarns "Aran Tweed" (100% wool; 88 yd./ 80m per 50g skein); Color: Turquoise (4847); 11 (12, 13, 15, 16, 17, 18) skeins

  NOTE: *This yarn is also sold under the "Kilcarra" and "Studio Donegal" labels.*

- US 8 (5mm) circular needle, 40" (100cm) length (or longer for larger sizes), *or size needed to obtain gauge*
- US 7 (4.5mm) circular needle, 40" (100cm) length (or longer for larger sizes), *or size needed to obtain gauge*
- US 8 (5mm) straight needles
- US 7 (4.5mm) double-pointed needles
- Cable needle
- Tapestry needle
- Stitch markers
- Stitch holders
- Safety pins
- 10 (10, 10, 10, 10, 11, 11) shank buttons, 1" (2.5cm)

ɡauɡe

18 sts × 24 rows = 4" (10cm) in St st on larger needles

24 sts × 26 rows = 4" (10cm) in 2 × 2 Ribbing on smaller needles

Knotted Cable panel (36 sts) measures 5.75" (14.5cm) across

pαττern noτes

For m1p, p2tog tbl, One-Row Buttonhole, w&t (short rows), cable cast-on, and three-needle bind-off techniques, please see the "Knitting Techniques" appendix.

2 × 2 Ribbing (rows)

(worked over a multiple of 4 sts + 2)

Row 1 (RS): *K2, p2; rep from * to last 2 sts, k2.

Row 2 (WS): *P2, k2; rep from * to last 2 sts, p2.

Rep these 2 rows for patt.

2 × 2 Ribbing (rnds)

(worked over a multiple of 4 sts)

Rnd 1: *K2, p2; rep from * to end of rnd.

Rep this rnd for patt.

Knotted Cable

Worked over 36 sts; see chart for details.

Instructions

Faux side seams are worked in garter stitch on this cardigan. Note that the Knotted Cable Chart begins on a WS row.

body

With smaller circular needle, CO 182 (202, 226, 246, 274, 294, 314) sts. Work for 4" (10cm) in 2 × 2 Ribbing ending with a WS row.

Dec Row (RS): Working in 2 × 2 Ribbing, dec 4 (8, 14, 18, 24, 28, 30) sts evenly spaced across row. 178 (194, 212, 228, 250, 266, 284) sts.

Next Row (WS): Switch to larger circular needle and k2, work Knotted Cable Chart over 36 sts beg with Row 1, *k6 (10, 14, 18, 24, 28, 32), k1 (seam st), k6 (10, 14, 18, 24, 28, 32), work Knotted Cable Chart*, k4 (4, 6, 6, 4, 4, 6), work Knotted Cable Chart, rep from * to *, k2.

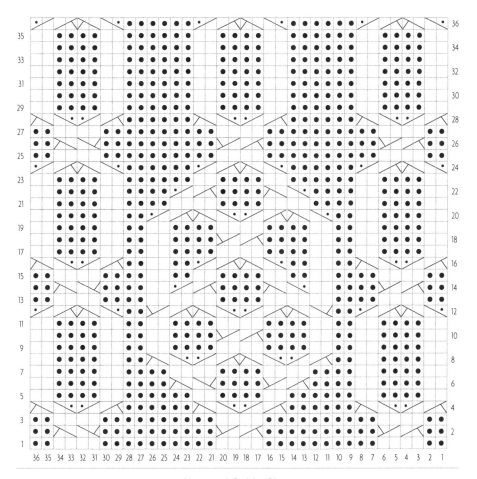

Knotted Cable Chart

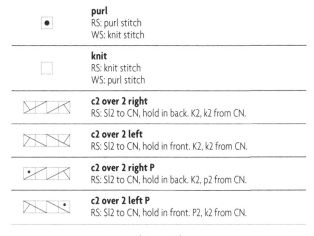

	purl
●	RS: purl stitch WS: knit stitch
	knit
☐	RS: knit stitch WS: purl stitch
	c2 over 2 right
	RS: Sl2 to CN, hold in back. K2, k2 from CN.
	c2 over 2 left
	RS: Sl2 to CN, hold in front. K2, k2 from CN.
	c2 over 2 right P
	RS: Sl2 to CN, hold in back. K2, p2 from CN.
	c2 over 2 left P
	RS: Sl2 to CN, hold in front. P2, k2 from CN.

Legend

Next Row (RS): P2, work Knotted Cable Chart, *p6 (10, 14, 18, 24, 28, 32), k1 (seam st), p6 (10, 14, 18, 24, 28, 32), work Knotted Cable Chart*, p4 (4, 6, 6, 4, 4, 6), work Knotted Cable Chart, rep from * to *, p2.

Cont to work in est'd patt until piece measures 8.5" (21.5cm), ending with a WS row.

Waist Shaping

Waist Dec Row (RS): *Work in patt to 2 sts before side seam st, p2tog, k1 (seam st), p2tog tbl; rep from * once. 4 sts dec'd.

Work Waist Dec Row every 6 (6, 4, 4, 4, 4, 4) rows 1 (1, 4, 4, 4, 4, 4) time(s), and then every 4 (4, 2, 2, 2, 2, 2) rows 4 (4, 3, 3, 3, 3, 3) times. 154 (170, 180, 196, 218, 234, 252) sts.

Work even in patt until piece measures 14.25" (36cm) ending with a WS row.

Bust Shaping

Bust Inc Row (RS): *Work in patt to side seam st, m1p, k1 (seam st), m1p; rep from * once. 4 sts inc'd.

Work Bust Inc Row every 8 (8, 6, 6, 6, 6, 6) rows 3 (3, 2, 2, 2, 2, 2) times and then every 0 (0, 4, 4, 4, 4, 4) rows 0 (0, 3, 3, 3, 3, 3) times. 170 (186, 204, 220, 242, 258, 276) sts.

Work even in patt until piece measures 21.5 (21.75, 22, 22.25, 21.75, 21.75, 21.75)"/54.5 (55, 56, 56.5, 55, 55, 55) cm ending with a WS row.

Divide for Armholes

Dividing Row (RS): Work 42 (46, 50, 54, 60, 64, 68) sts to side seam st; with new ball of yarn BO 1 st (seam st), with straight needles, work to left side seam; with circular needle, BO 1 st (seam st), work to end of row. 84 (92, 102, 110, 120, 128, 138) sts held for back on straight needle to be worked later.

Make note of the last row worked from chart.

You will now work each side of the front separately with 2 balls of yarn. The semicolon in each line indicates the division between left and right front.

Sleeve Shaping

Next Row (WS): Starting with right front, work in patt to end of row for both sides of front.

Sleeve Inc Row (RS): P1, m1p, work to end of left side; work right side to last st, m1p, p1.

Rep these 2 rows twice. 45 (49, 53, 57, 63, 67, 71) sts each side.

Sleeve Inc Row (WS): Using cable cast-on method, CO 3 sts, work to end of row; work to end of row.

Sleeve Inc Row (RS): CO 3 sts, work to end of row; work to end of row. 48 (52, 56, 60, 66, 70, 74) sts each side.

Work even until fronts measure 3 (3.5, 4, 4.5, 5, 5, 5.25)"/7.5 (9, 10, 11.5, 12.5, 12.5, 13.5) cm from CO underarm sts, ending with a WS row.

NOTE: *Read through neckline and shoulder shaping sections before knitting; shoulder shaping begins before neckline shaping is complete.*

Neckline Shaping

Next Row (RS): Work left front; BO 5 (5, 5, 5, 7, 7, 7) sts, work to end of row.

Next Row (WS): Work right front; BO 5 (5, 5, 5, 7, 7, 7) sts, work to end of row. 43 (47, 51, 55, 59, 63, 67) sts each side.

Neck Dec Row 1 (RS): Work to last 3 sts before neck edge, p2tog tbl, p1; p1, p2tog, work to end of row. 1 st dec'd each side.

Neck Dec Row 2 (WS): Work to last 3 sts before neck edge, k2tog, k1; k1, ssk, work to end of row. 1 st dec'd each side.

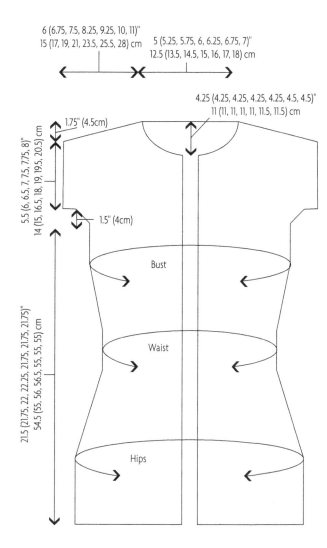

6 (6.75, 7.5, 8.25, 9.25, 10, 11)"
15 (17, 19, 21, 23.5, 25.5, 28) cm

5 (5.25, 5.75, 6, 6.25, 6.75, 7)"
12.5 (13.5, 14.5, 15, 16, 17, 18) cm

4.25 (4.25, 4.25, 4.25, 4.25, 4.5, 4.5)"
11 (11, 11, 11, 11, 11.5, 11.5) cm

1.75" (4.5cm)

5.5 (6, 6.5, 7, 7.5, 7.75, 8)"
14 (15, 16.5, 18, 19, 19.5, 20.5) cm

1.5" (4cm)

Bust

Waist

21.5 (21.75, 22, 22.25, 21.75, 21.75, 21.75)"
54.5 (55, 56, 56.5, 55, 55, 55) cm

Hips

NOTE: Bust, waist, and hip dimensions do NOT include buttonband.
Bust: 28.75 (32.25, 36.25, 40, 44.75, 48.25, 52.25)"
73 (82, 92, 101.5, 113.5, 122.5, 132.5) cm

Waist: 25.25 (28.75, 31, 34.5, 39.5, 43, 47)"
64 (73, 78.5, 87.5, 100.5, 109, 119.5) cm

Hips: 30.5 (34, 38, 41.5, 46.5, 50, 54)"
77.5 (86.5, 96.5, 105.5, 118, 127, 137) cm

Rep these 2 rows 2 (2, 2, 3, 3, 3, 3) times. 37 (41, 45, 47, 51, 55, 59) sts each side.

Work Neck Dec Row 1 (RS rows only) 4 (5, 5, 4, 4, 5, 5) times. 33 (36, 40, 43, 47, 50, 54) sts rem on each side.

At the same time, when piece measures 5.5 (6, 6.5, 7, 7.5, 7.75, 8)"/14 (15, 16.5, 18, 19, 19.5, 20.5) cm from CO underarm sts, shape shoulders as follows starting with a RS row.

Shoulder Shaping

You will work short rows to shape the shoulders. Work across both sides of front on every row.

*Rows 1 & 2: Work in patt; work to last 5 (6, 7, 7, 8, 8, 9) sts, w&t.

Rows 3 & 4: Work in patt; work to last 11 (12, 14, 14, 16, 17, 18) sts, w&t.

Rows 5 & 6: Work in patt; work to last 17 (18, 21, 21, 24, 26, 27) sts, w&t.

Rows 7 & 8: Work in patt; work to last 22 (24, 28, 29, 32, 35, 37) sts, w&t.

Rows 9 & 10: Work in patt; work to last 27 (31, 34, 37, 41, 44, 47) sts, w&t.

Next Row (RS): Work to end of row in patt.*

Place 33 (36, 40, 43, 47, 50, 54) sts from each shoulder on holder for three-needle bind-off.

back

With WS facing, reattach yarn to 84 (92, 102, 110, 120, 128, 138) sts held for back.

NOTE: Make sure you begin Knotted Cable Chart with the appropriate row from the chart.

Next Row (WS): Work all sts in patt.

Sleeve Inc Row (RS): P1, m1p, work to last st, m1p, p1. 86 (94, 104, 112, 122, 130, 140) sts.

Rep these 2 rows twice. 90 (98, 108, 116, 126, 134, 144) sts.

Sleeve Inc Row (WS): Using cable cast-on method, CO 3 sts, work to end of row.

Sleeve Inc Row (RS): CO 3 sts, work to end of row. 96 (104, 114, 122, 132, 140, 150) sts.

Work even in patt until back measures 5.5 (6, 6.5, 7, 7.5, 7.75, 8)"/14 (15, 16.5, 18, 19, 19.5, 20.5) cm from CO underarm sts, ending with a WS row.

Work short-row shoulder shaping as for front from * to *. After shoulder shaping is complete, place center 30 (32, 34, 36, 38, 40, 42) sts on holder for back of neck. You will join 33 (36, 40, 43, 47, 50, 54) sts from each shoulder using three-needle bind-off.

Finishing

joining shoulders

Fold front and back of cardigan so that the WS is facing you and the RS of the front and back are held together. Join front and back of each shoulder together using three-needle bind-off.

neckband

With smaller circular needle and RS facing, start at the right neck edge, and pick up and knit 5 (5, 5, 5, 7, 7, 7) bound-off sts, pick up and knit 15 (16, 17, 16, 17, 16, 17) sts up right side of neck, knit 30 (32, 34, 36, 38, 40, 42) sts held for back of neck, pick up and knit 15 (16, 17, 16, 17, 16, 17) sts down left side of neck, pick up and knit 5 (5, 5, 5, 7, 7, 7) bound-off sts. 70 (74, 78, 78, 86, 86, 90) sts.

Work in 2 × 2 Ribbing until work measures 7" (18cm) from picked-up sts.

BO all sts in patt.

button band

With smaller circular needle and RS facing, start at the top left neck edge, pick up and knit 3 sts for every 4 rows.

Next Row (WS): Work in 2 × 2 Ribbing, dec sts if necessary to ensure you have a multiple of 4 + 2.

Cont to work in 2 × 2 Ribbing until band measures 1.5" (4cm) from picked-up sts ending with a WS row.

BO all sts in patt.

buttonhole band

With smaller circular needle and RS facing, start at the bottom right edge, pick up and knit the same number of sts as for the button band.

NOTE: *If you wish to fasten the tunic with just a belt, then work this band as for the button band just worked.*

Next Row (WS): Work in 2 × 2 Ribbing.

Cont to work in 2 × 2 Ribbing until band measures 0.75" (2cm) from picked-up sts ending with a WS row.

Using safety pins, mark positions of buttonholes approx 4" (10cm) apart. Allow 3 sts before first buttonhole and 6 sts at end of band (*these sts are to work the final buttonhole as well as allowing 3 sts after final buttonhole*).

NOTE: *If desired, you may only work buttonholes as far as the collar so you can wear the collar open. If you do this, then adjust position of your final buttonhole accordingly.*

Buttonhole Row (RS): Work 3 sts in patt, *work One-Row Buttonhole, work to next buttonhole position; rep from * until 6 sts rem, work final One-Row Buttonhole.

Cont to work in 2 × 2 Ribbing until band measures 1.5" (4cm) from picked-up sts ending with a WS row.

BO all sts in patt.

Sew buttons in position opposite buttonholes. Sew top button on inside of collar so it can be buttoned and folded over (*if buttonholes are worked the full length of collar*).

sleeve edging

With dpns and RS facing, starting at underarm, pick up and knit 26 (26, 30, 32, 34, 36, 36) sts to top of shoulder, pick up and knit 26 (26, 30, 32, 34, 36, 36) sts to underarm. 52 (52, 60, 64, 68, 72, 72) sts.

Join to work in the rnd in 2 × 2 Ribbing for 6 rnds.

BO all sts in patt.

Rep for second sleeve.

belt

With dpns, CO 6 sts. Kfb 6 times. 12 sts.

Next Row: (K1, sl1 wyif) 6 times.

Rep this row until belt measures approx 46 (50, 52, 56, 60, 64, 68)"/117 (127, 132, 142, 152.5, 162.5, 172.5) cm.

Bind off as follows: K2tog, *k2tog, pass 2nd st over 1st st on RH needle; rep from * to end. Cut yarn and draw tail through final st.

belt loops

Measure 12.5" (32cm) from bottom of work. Mark this point at each side seam. Try on cardigan and belt to ensure you are happy with this location for the bottom of the belt loops.

At each marked spot, with dpns, pick up and knit 3 sts.

Next Row (WS): P1, k1, p1.

Next Row (RS): K1, p1, k1.

Work these 2 rows 4 more times and BO all sts.

Sew bound-off edge to work to form belt loop.

Weave in loose ends with tapestry needle.

Block sweater to dimensions given on schematic, taking care not to stretch out cables. Pinch cables into shape if necessary.

Glengesh

Cable-and-Lace Wrap

Flip the tail of this drapy wrap across your shoulder to create your very own stylish attitude. This warm and elegant shawl is long enough to wrap back across your shoulders and the subtle Donegal tweed adds depth to the textural interest. Wear it as a cozy scarf on a cold winter's day by wrapping it snugly around your neck.

Worked from the bottom up, short rows and decreases create a gentle curve to form a wrap that will stay in place. You can create another unique look with this versatile wrap by crossing the ends around your body and fastening at the back with a ribbon threaded through the eyelets to form a laced closure.

Finished measurements
14" (35.5cm) deep × 87" (221cm) long

Materials
- Donegal Yarns "Aran Tweed" (100% wool; 88 yd./ 80m per 50g skein); Color: Deep Red (4754); 8 skeins

  NOTE: This yarn is also sold under the "Kilcarra" and "Studio Donegal" labels.

- US 9 (5.5mm) circular needle, 60" (150cm) length, *or size needed to obtain gauge*
- Cable needle
- Tapestry needle
- Stitch markers

Gauge
Central Cable Panel, single repeat: 3" (7.5cm) deep × 3.75" (9.5cm) wide

Left or Right Cable-and-Lace Chart, single repeat: 1" (2.5cm) deep × 5.25" (13.5cm) wide

Gauge is given after blocking.

Pattern Notes
For short-row (w&t) and elastic bind-off instructions, please see the "Knitting Techniques" appendix.

Central Cable Pattern
Worked over 24 sts; see chart for details.

Left Cable-and-Lace Pattern
Worked over 22 sts; see chart for details.

Right Cable-and-Lace Pattern
Worked over 22 sts; see chart for details.

Lace Panel
Worked over 5 sts; see chart for details.

Instructions

This wrap is knit from the bottom up. Shaping is created using short rows and decreases.

CO 378 sts loosely.

NOTE: *Begin charts with Row 1, a WS row.*

Row 1 (WS): K1, work Left Cable-and-Lace Chart 8 times, work Central Cable Chart once, work Right Cable-and-Lace Chart 8 times, k1.

Row 2 (RS): P1, work Right Cable-and-Lace Chart 8 times, work Central Cable Chart once, work Left Cable-and-Lace Chart 8 times, p1.

Work in patt as set until you have worked the Right and Left Cable-and-Lace Charts 7 times, then work Rows 1–3 once more. Piece measures approx 7.5" (19cm).

Dec Row (RS): P1, [k1, ssk, k2tog, k1, work Lace Panel Chart beg with Row 2] 16 times, work Central Cable Chart, [work Lace Panel Chart beg with Row 2, k1, ssk, k2tog, k1] 16 times, p1. 314 sts.

Next Row (WS): K1, [k4, work Lace Panel Chart] 16 times, work Central Cable Chart, [work Lace Panel Chart, k4] 16 times, k1.

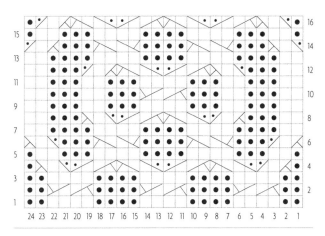

Central Cable Chart

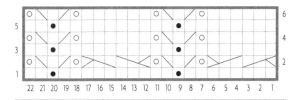

Left Cable-and-Lace Chart

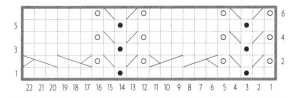

Right Cable-and-Lace Chart

Lace Panel Chart

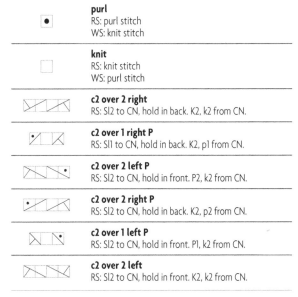

	purl RS: purl stitch WS: knit stitch
	knit RS: knit stitch WS: purl stitch
	c2 over 2 right RS: Sl2 to CN, hold in back. K2, k2 from CN.
	c2 over 1 right P RS: Sl1 to CN, hold in back. K2, p1 from CN.
	c2 over 2 left P RS: Sl2 to CN, hold in front. P2, k2 from CN.
	c2 over 2 right P RS: Sl2 to CN, hold in back. K2, p2 from CN.
	c2 over 1 left P RS: Sl2 to CN, hold in front. P1, k2 from CN.
	c2 over 2 left RS: Sl2 to CN, hold in front. K2, k2 from CN.

Legend to Central Cable Chart

	knit RS: knit stitch WS: purl stitch
	purl RS: purl stitch WS: knit stitch
	yo RS: yarn over
	k2tog RS: Knit two stitches together as one stitch.
	ssk RS: Slip one stitch as if to knit. Slip another stitch as if to knit. Insert LH needle into front of these 2 stitches and knit them together.
	c3 over 3 right RS: Sl3 to CN, hold in back. K3, k3 from CN.
	c3 over 3 left RS: Sl3 to CN, hold in front. K3, k3 from CN.
	Pattern Repeat

Legend to Cable-and-Lace and Lace Panel Charts

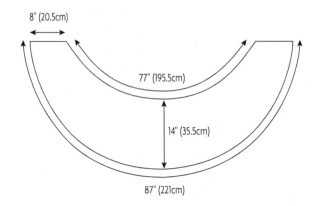

8" (20.5cm)

77" (195.5cm)

14" (35.5cm)

87" (221cm)

short-row shaping

See the "Knitting Techniques" appendix for details on how to work short rows, including wrap & turn (w&t).

Row 1 (RS): Work in patt to end of Central Cable Chart, work Lace Panel Chart once, k1, w&t.

Row 2 (WS): Work in patt to end of Central Cable Chart, work Lace Panel Chart once, k1, w&t.

Row 3 (RS): Work in patt 9 sts past previous turn (picking up and knitting wrap together with wrapped st when passed), w&t.

Row 4 (WS): Work in patt 9 sts past previous turn (picking up and knitting wrap together with wrapped st when passed), w&t.

Continue to work last 2 rows 14 more times.

Work 2 rows in patt, picking up remaining wraps.

Dec Row (RS): P1, [ssk, k2tog, work Lace Panel Chart] 16 times, work Central Cable Chart, [work Lace Panel Chart, ssk, k2tog] 16 times, p1. 250 sts.

Next Row (WS): K1, [p2, work Lace Panel Chart] 16 times, work Central Cable Chart, [work Lace Panel Chart, p2] 16 times, k1.

BO all sts using the elastic bind-off, work k2tog at center of each cable on Central Cable to prevent flaring.

Finishing

Weave in all ends using tapestry needle.

Block wrap to dimensions given on schematic. To open up the lacework, you need to stretch the lace panels open.

straboy

Men's Aran Hoodie

Hoodies are wonderfully versatile garments; snug and cozy with a laid-back, contemporary style. This pattern has a uniquely Irish take on the modern hoodie. Styled with a casual feel, this hoodie makes great use of traditional cable panels but is also suitable for even a modern Irish surfer after a cold day on the winter waters.

materials

- Donegal Yarns "Aran Tweed" (100% wool; 88 yd./ 80m per 50g skein); Color: Oatmeal (4585); 16 (18, 20, 22, 24) skeins

  NOTE: *This yarn is also sold under the "Kilcarra" and "Studio Donegal" labels.*

- US 8 (5mm) double-pointed needles
- US 7 (4.5mm) double-pointed needles
- US 8 (5mm) circular needle, 24" (60cm) length (or longer for larger sizes), *or size needed to obtain gauge*
- US 7 (4.5mm) circular needle, 24" (60cm) length (or longer for larger sizes)
- Cable needle
- Tapestry needle
- Stitch markers
- Waste yarn

size

To fit actual chest circumference up to: 35 (40, 44, 48, 52)"/89 (102, 112, 122, 132) cm

2–4" (5–10cm) of positive ease is recommended.

finished measurements

Chest circumference: 37.25 (42, 45.75, 50, 53.75)"/ 94.5 (107, 116, 127, 136.5) cm

Length: 30 (30.75, 31.25, 32, 32.75)"/ 76 (78, 79.5, 81.5, 83) cm

Size 42" (107 cm) modeled with 2.5" (6.5cm) of positive ease.

ɠauɠe

18 sts × 24 rows = 4" (10cm) in Moss st on larger needles

24 sts × 24 rows = 4" in Trinity st on larger needles

Braided Cable Panel, single repeat: 7.25" (18.5cm) across

paᴛᴛeʀɴ ɴoᴛes

For m1, three-needle bind-off, and grafting techniques, please see the "Knitting Techniques" appendix.

Trinity Stitch (rows)

(worked over a multiple of 4 sts + 2)

Row 1 (RS): Purl.

Row 2 (WS): K1, *(k1, p1, k1 into 1 st), p3tog; rep from * to last st, k1.

Row 3: Purl.

Row 4: K1, *p3tog, (k1, p1, k1 into 1 st); rep from * to last st, k1.

Trinity Stitch (rnds)

(worked over a multiple of 4 sts + 2)

Rnd 1: Purl.

Rnd 2: P1, *(p1, k1, p1 into 1 st), sssk; rep from * to last st, p1.

Rnd 3: Purl.

Rnd 4: P1, *sssk, (p1, k1, p1 into 1 st); rep from * to last st, p1.

Moss Stitch (rows)

(worked over an odd number of sts)

Row 1: *K1, p1; rep from * to last st, k1.

Rep this row for patt.

(worked over an even number of sts)

Row 1: *K1, p1; rep from * to end.

Row 2: *P1, k1; rep from * to end.

Rep these 2 rows for patt.

Moss Stitch (rnds)

(worked over an odd number of sts)

Rnd 1: *K1, p1; rep from * to last st, k1.

Rnd 2: *P1, k1; rep from * to last st, p1.

Rep these 2 rnds for patt.

Braided Cable Panel

Worked over 39 sts; see chart for details.

NOTE: *This chart begins on a WS row.*

Instructions

You will work the body and sleeves (separately) from the bottom in the round. At the yoke, you will join the pieces together and work as one piece.

body

You will work the front and back separately to form side slits and then join them to work in the rnd.

Back

*With smaller circular needle, CO 80 (92, 100, 112, 120) sts. Work 1 WS row in Moss st.

Working in Moss st, you will inc 1 st at each end of every row 2 times and then every RS row 2 times. Work increases as follows: Kfb, work to last 2 sts, kfb, k1, being sure to knit the purl sts and purl the knit sts to maintain patt. 88 (100, 108, 120, 128) sts.

Work 4 more rows in Moss st ending with a RS row.

Inc Row (WS): **Inc 12 sts as follows:** work 4 (8, 12, 14, 18) in Moss st, [m1, Moss st 7 (7, 7, 9, 9) sts] 4 (2, 2, 2, 2) times, [m1, Moss st 8 (8, 8, 8, 8) sts] 3 (7, 7, 7, 7) times, [m1, Moss st 7 (7, 7, 9, 9) sts] 4 (2, 2, 2, 2) times, m1, work in Moss st to end of row. 100 (112, 120, 132, 140) sts.

Set-up Row (RS): Switch to larger needle and work 4 (8, 12, 14, 18) sts in Moss st, work Braided Cable Panel Set-up Row, work 14 (18, 18, 26, 26) sts in Trinity st, work Braided Cable Panel Set-up Row, work 4 (8, 12, 14, 18) sts in Moss st.

Next Row (WS): Work 4 (8, 12, 14, 18) sts in Moss st, work Row 1 of Braided Cable Panel Chart, work 14 (18, 18, 26, 26) sts in Trinity st, work Row 1 of Braided Cable Panel Chart, work 4 (8, 12, 14, 18) sts in Moss st.

Cont to work in est'd patt until piece measures 4" (10cm) ending with a WS row.

Break yarn and set sts aside.*

Front

Work front from * to * as for back.

Body

NOTE: Initial Moss st panel is slipped to ensure pattern will match up when back is joined.

Starting with front, sl 4 (8, 12, 14, 18) sts, rejoin yarn, work rem front sts in est'd patt, pm for side seam,

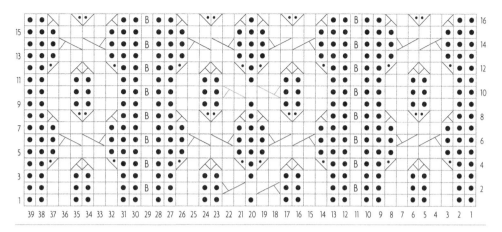

Braided Cable Panel Chart

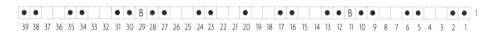

Braided Cable Panel Set-up Row Chart

●	**purl**	RS: purl stitch WS: knit stitch
	knit	RS: knit stitch WS: purl stitch
B	**knit tbl**	RS: knit stitch through back loop WS: purl stitch through back loop
	c3 over 2 right	RS: Sl2 to CN, hold in back. K3, k2 from CN.
	c2 over 1 left P	RS: Sl2 to CN, hold in front. P1, k2 from CN.
	c2 over 1 right P	RS: Sl1 to CN, hold in back. K2, p1 from CN.
	c2 over 2 right	RS: Sl2 to CN, hold in back. K2, k2 from CN.
	c2 over 2 left	RS: Sl2 to CN, hold in front. K2, k2 from CN.
	c3 over 2 left	RS: Sl3 to CN, hold in front. K2, k3 from CN.

Legend

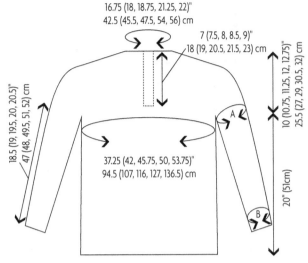

NOTE: Hood is not shown; dimensions are given in the pattern.

16.75 (18, 18.75, 21.25, 22)"
42.5 (45.5, 47.5, 54, 56) cm

7 (7.5, 8, 8.5, 9)"
18 (19, 20.5, 21.5, 23) cm

18.5 (19, 19.5, 20, 20.5)"
47 (48, 49.5, 51, 52) cm

10 (10.75, 11.25, 12, 12.75)"
25.5 (27, 29, 30.5, 32) cm

37.25 (42, 45.75, 50, 53.75)"
94.5 (107, 116, 127, 136.5) cm

A

B

20" (51cm)

A: 14.5 (15.75, 16, 18, 18.5)"/36.5 (40, 41, 45.5, 47) cm
B: 11 (11, 11.75, 12.25, 12.75)"/27.5 (27.5, 30, 31, 32) cm

work back sts in est'd patt, pm for end of rnd. 200 (224, 240, 264, 280) sts.

Cont to work in est'd patt until piece measures 20" (51cm), or desired length ending with an odd rnd.

Work in patt to 1 (3, 3, 4, 4) sts after side seam, place 2 (6, 6, 8, 8) sts just worked on waste yarn, work in patt to 1 (3, 3, 4, 4) sts after end of rnd, place 2 (6, 6, 8, 8) sts just worked on waste yarn. Place remaining (front and back) body sts aside on waste yarn to work later, do not break yarn. 98 (106, 114, 124, 132) sts front and back.

sleeves

NOTE: *When working Braided Cable Panel in the rnd, read all rows from right to left.*

With smaller dpns, CO 49 (51, 53, 55, 57) sts, pm for start of rnd, and join to work in the rnd taking care not to twist sts.

Work in Moss st for 9 rnds.

Inc Rnd: Work 8 (9, 10, 11, 12) sts in Moss st, m1, [work in Moss st for 7 sts, m1] 3 times, [work in Moss st for 6 sts, m1] 2 times, work in Moss st to end of rnd. 6 sts inc'd—55 (57, 59, 61, 63) sts.

Next Rnd: Switch to larger dpns, work 8 (9, 10, 11, 12) sts in Moss st, work Braided Cable Panel Chart, work 8 (9, 10, 11, 12) sts in Moss st to end of rnd.

Work Sleeve Inc Rnd [see below] every 12 (10, 10, 8, 8) rnds 6 (7, 4, 6, 3) times, then every 13 (11, 11, 9, 9) rnds 2 (3, 6, 7, 10) times. 16 (20, 20, 26, 26) sts inc'd—71 (77, 79, 87, 89) sts.

Sleeve Inc Rnd: End previous rnd 1 st before marker. M1, k1, sl m, k1, m1, work in est'd patt to end of rnd. Work new sts into Moss st patt.

Work in est'd patt until sleeve measures 18.5 (19, 19.5, 20, 20.5)" / 47 (48, 49.5, 51, 52) cm or desired length, ending with an even-numbered rnd.

Work 1 (2, 2, 3, 3) st(s) from start of rnd, place 2 (6, 6, 8, 8) sts just worked on waste yarn, break yarn and set sts aside. 69 (71, 73, 79, 81) sts.

Rep for second sleeve.

yoke

*The body and sleeves are now joined and worked in the rnd, continuing in pattern as established. You will knit 2 sts on **each** side of the raglan markers to create smooth seam lines. When decreasing in the braided cable panels, work sts in knit or purl to maintain pattern and discontinue each cable when too few sts remain to complete it.*

Set-up Rnd (Odd-numbered Rnd): Pm for start of rnd and raglan seam, k2, work in patt across front of body, pm for raglan seam, k2, work right sleeve in patt to last 2 sts, k2, pm for raglan seam, k2, work back of body in patt to last 2 sts, k2, pm for raglan seam, work left sleeve in patt to last 2 sts, k2. 334 (354, 374, 406, 426) sts.

Dec Rnd (Even-numbered Rnd): K2tog, (work in est'd patt to 2 sts before m, ssk, sm, k2tog) 3 times, work in est'd patt to 2 sts before m, ssk. 8 sts dec'd—326 (346, 366, 398, 418) sts.

Next Rnd: Work in patt to end of rnd.

Rep these 2 rnds 7 (7, 8, 8, 9) more times.

Work 1 more Dec Rnd. 262 (282, 294, 326, 338) sts.

Dividing the Neck

NOTE: The neck is divided at the center of the front panel (Trinity st panel). You will cast on extra stitches that will overlap at the front placket and begin working back on a WS row from this dividing point.

Work to end of first Braided Cable Panel, work 4 (4, 4, 8, 8) sts of Trinity st panel, turn work to WS, CO 6 (10, 10, 10, 10) sts, work to end of WS row *(odd-numbered row from chart)* in patt working new sts in Trinity st. 268 (292, 304, 336, 348) sts.

Dec Row (RS): Sl1, (work in patt to 2 sts before m, ssk, sm, k2tog) 4 times, work in patt to end of row. 8 sts dec'd—260 (284, 296, 328, 340) sts.

Next Row (WS): Sl1, work in est'd patt to end of row.

Work these 2 rows 20 (22, 23, 25, 26) more times, discontinuing cables as necessary and slipping first st each row. 100 (108, 112, 128, 132) sts.

hood

You will now work the hood in Trinity St only.

Inc Row (RS): Sl1, work Trinity st panel, m1, (purl to Trinity st panel, m1) twice. 3 sts inc'd—103 (111, 115, 131, 135) sts.

Work in Trinity st until hood measures 4" (10cm), ending on row 4 of patt.

Hood Inc Row 1 (RS): Sl1, (p1, k1, p1) into first st, work to last 2 sts, (p1, k1, p1) into 1 st, p1. 4 sts inc'd—107 (115, 119, 135, 139) sts.

Hood Inc Row 2 (WS): Sl1, kfb twice, work Trinity st to last 3 sts, kfb twice, k1. 4 sts inc'd—111 (119, 123, 139, 143) sts.

Cont in Trinity st until hood measures 8" (20.5cm), ending on row 4 of patt. Work Hood Inc Rows 1 & 2. 8 sts inc'd—119 (127, 131, 147, 151) sts.

Work even until hood measures approx. 13 (13.25, 13.5, 13.75, 14)"/33 (33.5, 34.5, 35, 35.5) cm ending with a WS row.

Dec Row (RS): Work 59 (63, 65, 73, 75) sts in patt, p2tog, work to end of row.

Place 59 (63, 65, 73, 75) sts on each end of circular needle, fold hood with RS facing each other, and BO using three-needle bind-off.

Finishing

Weave loose ends in with tapestry needle.

Graft underarm seams together.

Sew base of neckline band in place.

Block sweater to dimensions given on schematic.

Take care to block cables gently, pinching into shape if necessary.

Rossbeg (Girl's Cabled Yoke Cardigan)

rossbes

Girl's Cabled Yoke Cardigan

The warm orange tones of this "Soft Donegal" yarn will brighten up any little girl's wardrobe. Knitted from the top down, you can easily add length to create a long tunic style for your child to wear over leggings. Decorative and feminine, this cardigan is worked with two simple design elements, a braided cable and garter stitch. The braided cable portion of the yoke is knit first. Next, you pick up stitches to work the neckband and then pick up from the bottom of the yoke to finish knitting down the body. This garment is sized to fit a little more snugly than with standard hand knits; if your child likes her clothes to fit loosely, then go up a size.

size

To fit actual chest circumference up to: 21 (23, 25, 27, 29)"/53.5 (58.5, 63.5, 68.5, 73.5) cm

Suggested ages: 2 (4, 6, 8, 10) years

1–2" (2.5–5 cm) of positive ease is recommended.

finished measurements

Chest circumference (with buttonband closed): 22.25 (24, 26, 28.25, 30.25)"/56.5 (61, 66, 72, 77) cm

Length: 14 (15, 16, 17, 18)"/35.5 (38, 40.5, 43, 46) cm

Size 23.25" (59cm) modeled on a 2-year-old with 2" (5cm) of positive ease.

materials

- Donegal Yarns "Soft Donegal" (100% merino wool; 98 yd./90m per 50g skein); Color: Orange (5230); 5 (6, 7, 8, 9) skeins

  NOTE: *This yarn is also sold under the "Studio Donegal" label.*

- US 8 (5mm) straight needles, *or size needed to obtain gauge*
- US 7 (4.5mm) straight needles
- US 8 (5mm) double-pointed needles
- US 7 (4.5mm) double-pointed needles
- Cable needle
- Tapestry needle
- Stitch markers
- Waste yarn
- 6 (6, 7, 7, 8) toggle buttons, 1" (2.5cm)

gauge

17 sts × 24 rows = 4" (10cm) in St st on larger needles

18 sts × 32 rows = 4" (10cm) in garter st on smaller needles

Braided Cable Chart measures 2" (5cm) across worked flat on larger needles

pattern notes

For the m1 increase, One-Row Buttonhole, and the backwards loop cast-on techniques, please see the "Knitting Techniques" appendix.

Ridged Pattern (rows)

Rows 1, 3, and 5 (RS): Knit.

Rows 2 and 4 (WS): Purl.

Row 6 (WS): Knit.

Rep these 6 rows for patt.

Ridged Pattern (rnds)

Rnds 1–5: Knit.

Rnd 6: Purl.

Rep these 6 rnds for patt.

Garter Stitch (rows)

Knit all rows.

Garter Stitch (rnds)

Rnd 1: Knit.

Rnd 2: Purl.

Rep these 2 rnds for patt.

Braided Cable

Worked over 15 sts; see chart for details.

Instructions

You will start this piece by knitting the braided cable yoke flat. Then you pick up stitches, first for the neckline and then for the lower body, which is worked in one piece.

braided yoke

With larger straight needles, CO 15 sts.

Work Braided Cable Chart, beg with Row 1 (a RS row), until piece measures 16.25 (18.5, 19.75, 21.25, 22)"/ 41.5 (47, 50, 54, 56) cm.

BO all sts.

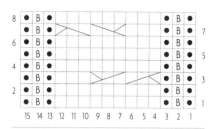

Braided Cable Chart

	purl
●	RS: purl stitch
	WS: knit stitch

	knit/purl tbl
B	RS: Knit stitch through back loop
	WS: Purl stitch through back loop

	knit
☐	RS: knit stitch
	WS: purl stitch

	c3 over 3 right
	RS: Sl3 to CN, hold in back. K3, k3 from CN.

	c3 over 3 left
	RS: Sl3 to CN, hold in front. K3, k3 from CN.

Legend

neckline

With RS of braided yoke facing and using larger straight needles, from right to left pick up and knit 70 (79, 85, 91, 94) sts evenly across top edge.

Next Row (WS): Knit.

Dec Row 1 (RS): *K3, k2tog; rep from * to last 5 (4, 5, 6, 4) sts, k to end. 13 (15, 16, 17, 18) sts dec'd— 57 (64, 69, 74, 76) sts.

Work in garter st until piece measures 0.5 (0.5, 0.75, 0.75, 1)"/1.5 (1.5, 2, 2, 2.5) cm from picked up sts, ending with a WS row.

Dec Row 2 (RS): *K5, k2tog; rep from * to last 1 (1, 6, 4, 6) st(s), k to end. 8 (9, 9, 10, 10) sts dec'd— 49 (55, 60, 64, 66) sts.

With smaller straight needles, work in garter st until piece measures 1 (1, 1.25, 1.25, 1.5)"/2.5 (2.5, 3.25, 3.25, 4) cm from picked up sts.

BO all sts.

lower yoke

With RS of yoke facing and using larger straight needles, pick up and knit 70 (79, 85, 91, 94) sts evenly along bottom edge.

Next Row (WS): Purl.

Inc Row 1 (RS): *K2, m1; rep from * to last 2 (1, 1, 1, 2) st(s), k to end. 34 (39, 42, 45, 46) sts inc'd— 104 (118, 127, 136, 140) sts.

Work in Ridged Pattern until piece measures 1 (1.25, 1.75, 1.75, 1.75)"/2.5 (3, 4.5, 4.5, 4.5) cm from picked up sts, ending with a WS row.

Inc Row 2 (RS): [K2, m1] 49 (29, 5, 11, 19) times, [k3, m1] 1 (19, 38, 37, 33) time(s), k to end. 50 (48, 43, 48, 52) sts inc'd—154 (166, 170, 184, 192) sts.

Work in Ridged Pattern until piece measures 2 (2.75, 3.5, 3.75, 3.75)"/5 (7, 9, 9.5, 9.5) cm from picked up sts, ending with a WS row.

Dividing for Sleeves

Next Row (RS): K22 (24, 25, 28, 29) sts; place next 32 (34, 34, 36, 38) sts on waste yarn; using back- wards loop cast-on method, CO 4 (4, 6, 6, 8) sts; k 46 (50, 52, 56, 58) sts for back; place next 32 (34, 34, 36, 38) sts on waste yarn; CO 4 (4, 6, 6, 8) sts; k to end of row. 98 (106, 114, 124, 132) sts.

body

Next Row (WS): Purl.

Inc Row (RS): Inc 18 sts evenly spaced across row. 116 (124, 132, 142, 150) sts.

Begin the Braided Cable Chart in the next row with Row 2 (a WS row) from chart.

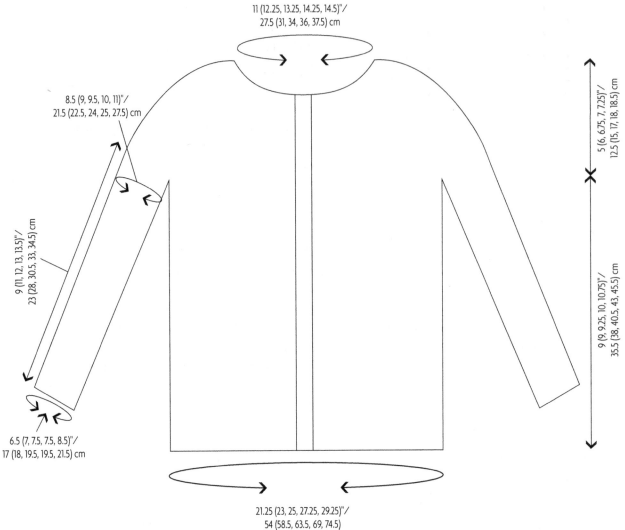

11 (12.25, 13.25, 14.25, 14.5)"/
27.5 (31, 34, 36, 37.5) cm

8.5 (9, 9.5, 10, 11)"/
21.5 (22.5, 24, 25, 27.5) cm

5 (6, 6.75, 7, 7.25)"/
12.5 (15, 17, 18, 18.5) cm

9 (11, 12, 13, 13.5)"/
23 (28, 30.5, 33, 34.5) cm

9 (9, 9.25, 10, 10.75)"/
35.5 (38, 40.5, 43, 45.5) cm

6.5 (7, 7.5, 7.5, 8.5)"/
17 (18, 19.5, 19.5, 21.5) cm

21.25 (23, 25, 27.25, 29.25)"/
54 (58.5, 63.5, 69, 74.5)
NOTE: Dimensions shown do not include buttonband.

Cable Set-up Row (WS): P7 (8, 9, 10, 11), work Braided Cable Chart, p14 (16, 18, 21, 23), work Braided Cable Chart, p14 (16, 18, 20, 22), work Braided Cable Chart, p14 (16, 18, 21, 23), work Braided Cable Chart, p to end of row.

Cont to work in est'd patt until cardigan measures 8 (8, 8.25, 9, 9.75)"/20.5 (20.5, 21, 23, 25) cm from underarm, ending with a WS row.

Next Row (RS): Switch to smaller straight needles and *k to Braided Cable, k5, k2tog, k1, ssk, k5, rep from * 3 times, k to end of row. 8 sts dec'd.

Cont in garter st for 1" (2.5cm).

BO all sts.

sleeves

With dpns, starting at center of underarm, pick up and knit 2 (2, 3, 3, 4) sts, place 32 (34, 34, 36, 38) sts from waste yarn on dpns and cont to work in Ridged Pattern, pick up and knit 2 (2, 3, 3, 4) sts to complete rnd, pm for start of rnd. 36 (38, 40, 42, 46) sts.

Work in Ridged Pattern for 15 (19, 21, 17, 17) rnds.

Sleeve Dec Rnd: K1, k2tog, work to last 3 sts, ssk, k1. 2 sts dec'd.

Rep these 16 (20, 22, 18, 18) rnds 2 (2, 2, 3, 3) more times. 30 (32, 34, 34, 38) sts. *If sleeve dec rnd falls on Ridge Pattern rnd, then work dec rnd on rnd **before** ridge.*

Cont to work in patt until sleeve measures 8 (10, 11, 12, 12.5)"/20.5 (25.5, 28, 30.5, 32) cm from underarm.

With smaller dpns, work in garter st for 1" (2.5cm).

BO all sts in patt.

Rep for second sleeve.

Finishing

button band

On left front of cardigan, with smaller straight needles and RS facing, working from top to bottom, pick up and knit 64 (68, 72, 76, 82) sts.

Work in garter st until band measures 1" (2.5cm) from picked up sts ending with a RS row.

BO all sts in patt.

buttonhole brand

On right front of cardigan, with smaller straight needles and RS facing, working from bottom to top, pick up and knit 64 (68, 72, 76, 82) sts.

Knit 3 rows.

Buttonhole Row (RS): K2, [work One-Row Buttonhole, k8 (8, 7, 8, 7)] 1 (5, 4, 2, 4) time(s), [work One-Row Buttonhole, k7 (0, 6, 7, 6)] 4 (0, 2, 4, 3) times, work final One-Row Buttonhole, knit to end.

Work in garter st until buttonhole band measures 1" (2.5cm) from picked up sts ending with a RS row.

BO all sts in patt.

Weave in loose ends with a tapestry needle.

Sew buttons in position opposite buttonholes.

Block cardigan to dimensions given in schematic. Take care to block cables gently.

new directions: the hand dyers

In the first three sections of this book, I looked at the mills that have been operating in Ireland for many generations. More recently, another breed of fiber activity has been developing here: the hand dyers. Hand dyers approach textiles from a very different angle than the mills. They playfully experiment with color and although they are businesses, they strongly emphasize having fun with their yarn. Such businesses frequently grow organically out of a personal hobby. Several hand dyers are operating in Ireland, and in this section I feature the yarns of two of them: the Dublin Dye Company and Hedgehog Fibres. (Additional listings of other Irish hand dyers are in the "Yarn Availability and Substitutions" appendix.)

Dublin Dye Company

Several years ago, Lisa Sisk, owner of the Dublin yarn shop This is Knit, took a dyeing workshop. She enjoyed it so much that she wanted to start teaching dyeing workshops in her own shop. So she ordered a large amount of yarn and dyes from Canada and started teaching. Two of her students in the first class, Yvonne McSwiney and Elana Kehoe, loved hand dyeing as much as Lisa did. Before long, they were helping Lisa dye in larger quantities and selling the finished yarn through This is Knit under the label "Dublin Dye Company." At the time, all of the dyeing was done in a room above the yarn shop, which worked well because there was plenty of space.

A few years later, This is Knit moved to a shopping center in downtown Dublin. However, space was at a premium so the yarn dyeing part of the business could not move with the shop. At this point, either the yarn dyeing business would close down entirely or someone else would have to take it over. This is when Elana and Yvonne stepped in.

Dublin Dye Company moved into a converted, detached garage next to Elana's house, known as "The Cottage." This space was ideal for their dyeing operation due to its small kitchenette and ample space for drying the dyed yarn. Due to Ireland's damp climate, drying is a big issue—good drying weather is rare and to be taken advantage of!

Both Elana and Yvonne have a strong preference for natural materials, with wool being their predominant fiber choice. They use acid dyes because their low pH is needed when dyeing protein fiber (such as wool) since wool is very sensitive to high pH levels. This does not mean caustic acid dyes though. Even vinegar is acidic enough to lower the pH.

Lisa had originally bought so much yarn and dye that the company has only recently needed to restock supplies. They are now sourcing new suppliers and are looking to the UK for their new yarn. The logistics of hand dyeing have confined them to offering primarily sock- and lace-weight yarns. However, as they hope to expand into a larger commercial business, they are working on methods of increasing their capacity so that they can dye dk weight yarn in quantities sufficient to knit an entire garment. This will reduce some of the issues involved in knitting a project from yarn with different dye lots.

Elana and Yvonne dye in a wide range of colors, although they are currently enjoying the subtleties of semi-solid dyes, in which different shades of the same color create a depth of color that allows the texture of the knitting to shine through. Although they enjoy playing with color and developing new variations, they also create a range of colorways that are readily reproducible.

Currently, Dublin Dye Company yarn is sold through This is Knit, both at its retail store and on its website. They also sell their hand-dyed yarn on Etsy at www.etsy.com/shop/dublindyeco. Up to this point, their business has developed organically and they hope it will continue to do so in the future.

Hedgehog Fibres

Set in Glanmire, a hilly suburb of Cork City, Hedgehog Fibres is run out of Beata Jezekova's home. With her little dog running at your feet and hens clucking in the run behind the house, it feels much more rural than its location would suggest. Much of her home is devoted to fiber and yarn, making it a haven for yarn lovers.

Beata hard at work wringing out yarn.

She quickly discovered that she had quite a talent for it, creating subtle colorways with multiple colors. Rather than looking for new work, Beata decided to give hand dyeing a go as a business and set up Hedgehog Fibres.

Although Hedgehog Fibres is still run out of Beata's house, she now has someone helping her once a week with twisting and tagging the yarn and fiber. Beata provides weekly website updates in which she announces when a new batch of hand-dyed yarns are available to buy. In her Etsy webshop (www.etsy.com/shop/hedgehogfibres), you'll find a very distinctive color palette. The colors are subtle, well blended, and tend towards neutral and darker colors. Some fibers and yarns are so popular that they sell out within hours of going live on Etsy.

Beata has a unique approach to dyeing which creates a finished product that she feels is closer to batik than *dip dyeing* (yarn is dipped into several different dye pots). For a semi-solid colorway, she dips the yarn into two different colors. However, for some of

Beata spinning with her signature "Fly Along" tattoo.

Beata moved to Cork in 2005 from Bratislava, Slovakia, and says that the warmth of the Irish people and the beauty of the countryside make her feel that this is her home now. A few years after moving to Ireland, Beata lost her job, which pushed her to begin a yarn-dyeing company. She had recently begun knitting and loved knitting with hand-dyed yarn. However, she couldn't afford to buy the oftentimes expensive hand-dyed yarns, so she decided to try dyeing yarn herself.

A selection of Hedgehog Fibres yarns.

This is a sampling of some Hedgehog Fibres roving for spinners.

her more complex colors, she may use six (or even more) different dyes on the same skein of yarn.

She applies dye in a random manor to avoid excessive pooling. This means that when her yarn is knitted up, you will get a much more even distribution of color than is common with many hand-dyed yarns. However, the random application of dye does have a downside: it makes exact replication of the colorways very difficult to produce. This means that if you are knitting a larger garment out of several hanks of yarn, then you should alternate skeins every couple of rows so the colors will blend together more smoothly.

After the yarn is dyed, Beata uses citric acid to set the color so it will last (and to minimize excessive bleeding when washing the yarn). Finally, the yarn is air dried. It is quite a sight for yarn lovers to see the multiple hanks of beautiful hand-dyed yarn stretched out on a line to dry!

As well as dyeing yarn, Beata also dyes fiber. Evidence of the increased popularity of spinning, fiber is now a very popular product in her shop. Due to the nature of fiber, it cannot be dyed in the same way as yarn. Instead, the dry dye powder is sprinkled on the fiber, which is then placed in a pot with citric acid and heated.

Beata sources her materials from around the world. Her yarn and fiber come primarily from China, although some of her silk comes from India. She is very careful to source well-spun yarn, sometimes even getting it custom spun to meet her exacting requirements. Unfortunately, I was only able to feature one of her many yarns in this book, but she uses a wide variety of weights and yarn types. Yarn weights range from lace weight to worsted, with fibers that include yak, bluefaced leicester, silk, alpaca, merino, and cashmere. She offers something for every taste and all of her products are very hard to resist!

NOTE: For information on where to buy each of these hand-dyed yarns, please refer to the "Yarn Availability and Substitutions" appendix.

Dalkey (Cowl and Fingerless Mittens)

dublin dye company

Dalkey: Cowl and Fingerless Mittens

Elegant and cozy, a cowl is a very easy way to keep your neck warm without adding the bulk of a scarf. The cable-and-lace pattern used for this cowl is fun to knit and gently entwines its way around your neck. Two different sizes are given for this cowl. The larger, slouchier style is shown in the photos; it looks great worn with a brooch to fold the excess material. This larger cowl is much easier to take on and off over the head. For a more fitted cowl, choose the smaller size and it will sit snugly around your neck; take care though to use the elastic bind-off so that you have plenty of stretch to get the cowl over your head.

Fingering-weight yarn creates nice, lightweight fingerless mittens that you can use for days when the weather turns a little cooler. A single cable-and-lace panel (which matches the all-over pattern on the cowl) provides visual interest without being overwhelming. The small amount of yarn used for these mittens means you can easily knit them from the remains of the hank used for your cowl.

size

Cowl—To fit actual neck circumference up to: All sizes, fitted (All sizes, slouchy)

Mittens—To fit actual hand circumference up to: 7 (7.5, 8)"/18 (19, 20.5) cm

finished measurements

Finished cowl sizes: 17 (22.5)"/43 (57) cm

Shown in size 22.5" (57cm), worn with several inches of positive ease. For a fitted cowl, work smaller size.

Finished mitten circumference: 7.25 (7.75, 8.5)"/18.5 (19.5, 21.5) cm

Shown in size 7.75" (19.5cm) with 0.5" (1.5cm) positive ease.

materials

- Dublin Dye Company "Merino Sock" (100% super-wash merino wool; 437 yd./400m per 100g skein); Raspberry; 1 (1) skein will complete both cowl and mittens; actual cowl yardage: 175 (230) yd./160 (210) m; actual mitten yardage: 125 (145, 165) yd./115 (130, 155) m
- Cowl: US 3 (3.25mm) circular needle, 16" (40cm) length, *or size needed to obtain gauge*
- Mittens: US 3 (3.25mm) double-pointed needles, *or size needed to obtain gauge*
- Cable needle
- Stitch marker
- Tapestry needle
- Waste yarn

gauge

Cowl: 34 sts × 40 rows = 4" (10cm) in Cable-and-Lace Pattern, slightly stretched

Mittens: 27 sts × 40 rows = 4" (10cm) in St st

pattern notes

For m1, M1R, M1L, the elastic bind-off, and backwards loop cast-on instructions, please see the "Knitting Techniques" appendix.

Cable-and-Lace Pattern (for cowl)

Worked in rnds over a multiple of 12 sts; see chart for details.

Note that on Rnds 11 and 23, the final 3 sts are borrowed from the start of the next rnd. However, do **not** move the marker indicating start of rnd.

Cable-and-Lace Panel (for mittens)

Worked over 4 sts to begin; see chart for details.

Move markers out on each side on Rnds 10 and 13.

1 × 1 Ribbing (for mittens)

(worked over a multiple of 2 sts)

Rnd 1: K1, p1; rep to end of rnd.

Rep Rnd 1 for patt.

Cowl Instructions

With circular needle, CO 132 (176) sts, pm for start of rnd, join to work in the rnd taking care not to twist sts.

Knit 5 rnds.

Inc Rnd: [K3, m1, k8] 12 (16) times. 144 (192) sts.

Work Rnds 1–24 of Cable-and-Lace Chart twice. Then work Rnds 1–9 once. (57 rnds total worked from chart)

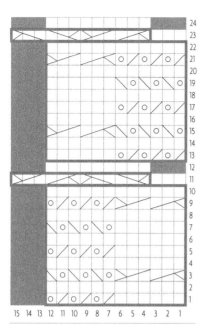

Cable-and-Lace Chart

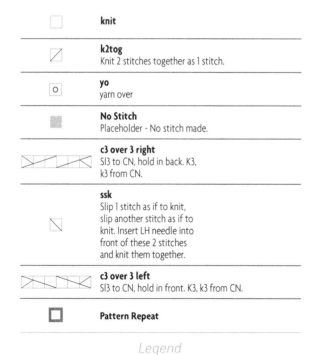

	knit
	k2tog Knit 2 stitches together as 1 stitch.
	yo yarn over
	No Stitch Placeholder - No stitch made.
	c3 over 3 right Sl3 to CN, hold in back. K3, k3 from CN.
	ssk Slip 1 stitch as if to knit, slip another stitch as if to knit. Insert LH needle into front of these 2 stitches and knit them together.
	c3 over 3 left Sl3 to CN, hold in front. K3, k3 from CN.
	Pattern Repeat

Legend

Dec Rnd: [K2, k2tog, k8] 12 (16) times. 132 (176) sts.

Knit 5 rnds.

BO all sts using the elastic bind-off, so cowl fits easily over head.

Finishing

Using tapestry needle, weave in all ends.

Block cowl, opening up lace panels.

Fingerless Mittens Instructions

RIGHT MITTEN

Using dpns, CO 48 (52, 56) sts, divide over 3 needles, and join to work in the rnd (taking care not to twist sts).

Knit 3 rnds.

Work in 1 × 1 Ribbing until work measures 2 (2.25, 2.5)"/5 (5.5, 6.5) cm allowing edge to roll.

Thumb Gusset

Right Mitten Set-up Rnd: K34 (37, 40), pm, work Cable-and-Lace Panel Chart, pm, knit to end of rnd, sm, m1, place new m. 51 (55, 59) sts. Final 2 markers mark gusset.

**Work 3 (2, 2) rnds in patt.

Inc Rnd: Work in patt to gusset m, sm, M1L, k to m, M1R, sm, work in patt to end of rnd. 53 (57, 61) sts.

Rep these 4 (3, 3) rnds 5 (0, 1) more time(s) and then work Inc Rnd every 0 (4, 4) rnds 0 (6, 6) times. 63 (69, 75) sts. 13 (15, 17) sts between gusset markers.

NOTE: *While working the Cable-and-Lace Panel Chart, st count will increase by 2 on Rnd 13 and decrease by 2 on Rnd 21.*

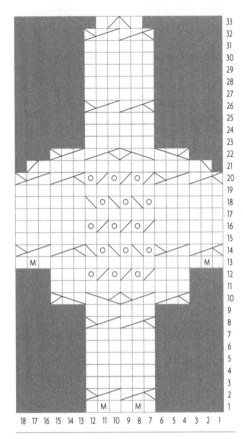

Cable-and-Lace Panel Chart

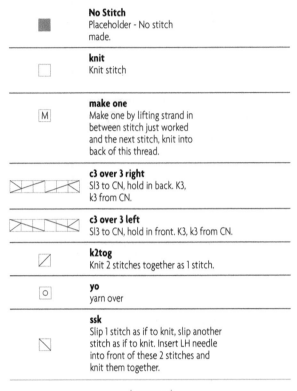

	No Stitch Placeholder - No stitch made.
	knit Knit stitch
M	**make one** Make one by lifting strand in between stitch just worked and the next stitch, knit into back of this thread.
	c3 over 3 right Sl3 to CN, hold in back. K3, k3 from CN.
	c3 over 3 left Sl3 to CN, hold in front. K3, k3 from CN.
	k2tog Knit 2 stitches together as 1 stitch.
O	**yo** yarn over
	ssk Slip 1 stitch as if to knit, slip another stitch as if to knit. Insert LH needle into front of these 2 stitches and knit them together.

Legend

Hand

Knit to first gusset marker, remove m, place next 13 (15, 17) sts on waste yarn to be worked later for thumb, CO 1 st using backwards loop cast-on method, work in patt to end of rnd. 51 (55, 59) sts.

Work in patt until mitten measures 3.5 (3.75, 4)"/ 9 (9.5, 10) cm from top of wrist ribbing. When chart is complete, continue in St st. 49 (53, 57) sts.

NOTE: *St count decreases by 2 on Rnd 33 of Cable-and-Lace Panel Chart.*

Work 1 rnd in 1 × 1 Ribbing and dec 1 st at end of rnd. 48 (52, 56) sts.

Work 3 more rnds in 1 × 1 Ribbing.

Knit 3 rnds.

BO all sts loosely.**

Thumb

Place 13 (15, 17) thumb gusset sts on dpns. Rejoin yarn, knit all sts, and pick up and knit 3 sts from CO st at base of thumb. 16 (18, 20) sts.

Knit 2 (4, 6) rnds.

Work 4 rnds in 1 × 1 Ribbing.

Knit 3 rnds.

BO all sts loosely.

left mitten

Cast on and work as for right mitten to beginning of thumb gusset.

Left Mitten Set-up Rnd: K10 (11, 12), pm, work Cable-and-Lace Panel Chart, pm, knit to end of rnd, sm, m1, pm. 51 (55, 59) sts.

Work from ** to ** as for right mitten.

Finishing

Using tapestry needle, weave in all ends.

Block mittens, making sure to open up central lace panels.

Rathcooney (Fingerless Mittens and Hat)

hedgehog fibres

Rathcooney: Fingerless Mittens and Hat

The elegant cocoon stitch flows organically into the ribbing for these fingerless mittens and hat. The soft and luxurious Hedgehog Fibres "Silk Merino Singles" makes this hat and mitten set a pleasure to knit and to wear. The thickness of the knitted fabric makes the mittens in particular wonderful for colder weather, while the tidy, neat fit of the hat creates a timeless elegance. The hand-dyed yarn adds sheen and subtle color to this design and the wonderful stitch definition enhances the texture of the pattern.

size

Mittens—to fit actual hand circumference up to:
7 (8.25, 9.5)"/18 (21, 24) cm

Hat—to fit actual head circumference up to: 20 (22, 24)"/51 (56, 61) cm

finished measurements

Hand circumference: 6.5 (7.75, 9)"/16.5 (19.5, 23) cm
Size 7.75" (19.5 cm) modeled with 0.5" (1.5cm) positive ease.
Finished Hat Size: 18 (19.25, 21.75)"/45.5 (49, 55) cm
Size 19.25" (49cm) modeled with 2" (5cm) negative ease.

materials

- Hedgehog Fibres Silk Merino singles (50% silk, 50% merino wool; 164 yd./150m per 100g skein); Color: Winter Thaw; 1 (1, 2) skein(s) for mittens; 1 (1, 2) skeins for hat
- US 6 (4mm) double-pointed needles, *or size needed to obtain gauge*
- US 7 (4.5mm) double-pointed needles (for applied I-cord on hat)
- Stitch markers
- Waste yarn
- Tapestry needle

gauge

Mittens and Hat: 25 sts × 30 rows = 4" (10cm) in Ribbing Pattern on smaller dpns, slightly stretched
Mittens and Hat: 28 sts × 32 rows = 4" (10cm) in Cocoon Stitch Pattern on smaller dpns

Pattern Notes

For m1p, backwards loop cast-on, I-cord bind-off, and applied I-cord instructions, please see the "Knitting Techniques" appendix.

Ribbing Pattern (for mittens and hat)

(worked in rnds over a multiple of 8 sts)

Rnd 1: (P5, k1, p1, k1) rep to end of rnd.

Rep Rnd 1 for patt.

Cocoon Stitch Pattern (for mittens and hat)

Worked in rnds over a multiple of 8 sts; see chart for details.

Rnds 1–3: (P5, k1, p1, k1) rep to end of rnd.

Rnd 4: (Sl 3 p-wise, p2tog, pass 3 sl sts over, k1, m1p, [p1, yo, p1] into 1 st, m1p, k1) rep to end of rnd.

Rnds 5–9: (P1, k1, p5, k1) rep to end of rnd.

Rnd 10: (M1p, [p1, yo, p1] into 1 st, m1p, k1, sl 3 p-wise, p2tog, pass 3 sl sts over, k1) rep to end of rnd.

Rnds 11–12: (P5, k1, p1, k1) rep to end of rnd.

Fingerless Mittens Instructions

Using smaller dpns, CO 40 (48, 56) sts, divide over 3 needles taking care not to divide st patt, join to work in the rnd.

Work Cocoon Stitch Chart for 24 rnds total.

Thumb Gusset

Set-up Rnd: Work in Ribbing Pattern over first 16 sts, p4, k1, pm, m1p, p1, m1p, pm, k1, work in Ribbing Pattern to end of rnd. 42 (50, 58) sts.

Continue to work in Ribbing Pattern as est'd, purling sts between markers, for 2 (3, 3) rnds.

Inc Rnd: Work to m, sm, m1p, p to m, m1p, sm, work in Ribbing Pattern to end of rnd. 44 (52, 60) sts.

Rep last 3 (4, 4) rnds 0 (4, 5) more times, then work Inc Rnd every 4 (0, 0) rnds 3 (0, 0) times. 52 (60, 70) sts. 13 (13, 15) sts between m.

Hand

Work in Ribbing Pattern to m, remove m, place next 13 (13, 15) sts on waste yarn to be worked later for thumb, CO 1 st using backwards loop cast-on method, work in Ribbing Pattern to end of rnd. 40 (48, 56) sts.

Work in Ribbing Pattern for 0 (0, 2) rnds.

Work 12 rows of Cocoon Stitch Chart.

BO all sts using I-cord bind-off.

Cocoon Stitch Chart

	8	7	6	5	4	3	2	1	
12		•		•	•	•	•	•	
11		•		•	•	•	•	•	
10	▨	▨	/⅀\		\⅃/				
9		•	•	•	•	•		•	
8		•	•	•	•	•		•	
7		•	•	•	•	•		•	
6		•	•	•	•	•		•	
5		•	•	•	•	•		•	
4	▨			\⅃/		/⅀\	▨		
3		•		•	•	•	•	•	
2		•		•	•	•	•	•	
1		•		•	•	•	•	•	

Cocoon Stitch Chart

Legend

•	**purl**	purl stitch
☐	**knit**	knit stitch
/⅀\	**k5tog**	Sl3 sts p-wise, k2tog, pass 3 sl sts over
\⅃/	**m5 sts in one**	M1p, (p1, yo, p1) into 1 st, m1p
▨	**No stitch**	Placeholder - No stitch made.

Legend

Thumb

Place 13 (13, 15) thumb gusset sts on dpns, rejoin yarn, p13 (13, 15) sts, pick up and purl 3 sts in CO st at base of thumb. 16 (16, 18) sts.

Purl 4 rnds.

BO all sts using I-cord bind-off.

Rep all instructions for second mitten.

Finishing

Work applied I-cord around bottom CO edge of mitten.

Using tapestry needle, weave in all ends.

Block mittens gently.

Hat Instructions

Brim

Using smaller dpns, CO 112 (120, 136) sts, divide over 3 needles taking care not to divide st patt repeats, pm for start of rnd, join to work in the rnd.

Work the Cocoon Stitch Chart for 24 total rnds.

head

Work in Ribbing Pattern until hat measures 5.5 (5.75, 6.25)"/14 (14.5, 16) cm from CO edge.

CROWN

Pm at the end of each Ribbing Pattern rep to mark dec points. 14 (15, 17) m placed (includes beg of rnd m).

Dec Rnd 1: [P2tog, work in patt to m, sm] 14 (15, 17) times. 98 (105, 119) sts.

Next Rnd: Work sts as they appear.

Work these 2 rnds 3 more times. 56 (60, 68) sts.

Dec Rnd 2: [K2tog, p1, k1] 14 (15, 17) times. 42 (45, 51) sts.

Remove all m except end of rnd m.

Dec Rnd 3: [K2tog, k1] 14 (15, 17) times. 28 (30, 34) sts.

Dec Rnd 4: [K2tog] 14 (15, 17) times. 14 (15, 17) sts

Dec Rnd 5: [K2tog] 7 (7, 8) times, k0 (1, 1). 7 (8, 9) sts.

Break yarn. With tapestry needle, draw yarn tail through final sts, pull tight, and weave into position.

Finishing

Using larger dpns, work applied I-cord around CO brim of hat.

Using tapestry needle, weave in all ends.

Block hat gently.

knitting techniques

casting on

If you have a preferred method of casting on, use that in your project. When no specific cast-on is mentioned in the pattern, then the longtail cast-on is my method of choice because it creates a nice edge to the work. Several other specialized cast-on methods are also described here and they are called for when needed in a pattern.

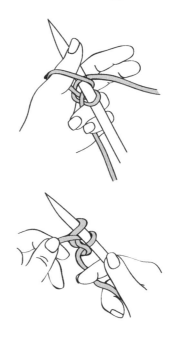

Backwards Loop Cast-On

Begin by placing a slip knot on your needle (if you are not working with established knitting). *With your thumb, scoop working yarn from underneath to create a loop. Lift this loop onto the needle, then slide out your thumb and pull working yarn to tighten up st; rep from * until desired number of sts have been cast on.

*If you are casting on with sts already on the needle, then you should began at *.*

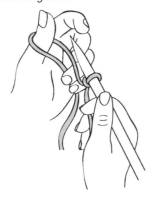

Cable Cast-On

If starting with no sts on needle, create slip knot, knit into slip knot, place st created from RH to LH needle. *Knit into the gap between the first 2 sts, slip new st created from RH to LH needle; rep from * until desired number of sts have been cast on.

*If you are casting on with sts already on the needle, then you should began at *.*

I-cord Cast-On

CO 3 sts, *kfb, k2, sl 3 sts onto LH needle, rep from * until desired number of sts have been worked plus 2. Sl 3 sts to LH needle, k2tog, k1, sl 2 to LH needle, k2tog. Sl rem st back to LH needle before beginning work.

NOTE: The first row after this cast on is sometimes loose. You can try knitting into the back loops of the sts on the first row to tighten up the sts. You may want to work a trial run of this cast-on and practice getting the sts as tight as possible.

Longtail Cast-On

Begin work by leaving a long tail. Typically, you will need a tail that is about 3 or 4 times the length you wish to cast on. This cast-on uses only 1 needle held in front of you as you work.

1. Create slip knot and tighten it on your needle. Keep working yarn to your right and the long yarn tail to your left.

2. With your left hand and the yarn tail, bring your thumb from behind the yarn, scoop it up, slide loop created onto the needle. Leave your thumb in place.

3. With right hand and working yarn, bring yarn around under the needle and wrap it on top (as though you were knitting a st). Keep holding this yarn in place.

4. With your left thumb still in the first loop, lift this thumb over the end of the needle, scooping the initial loop you created over the second loop made. Tighten the ends of the yarn until you are happy with the tension of the st.

Continue to repeat steps 2–4 until you have the correct number of sts on the needle.

Provisional Cast-On (Crochet Method)

This cast-on method uses waste yarn and a crochet hook to create a crochet chain that wraps a stitch around your knitting needle at the same time. You do not need to know how to crochet to use this method.

1. Make a slip knot with waste yarn and place on crochet hook.

2. Hold crochet hook above and perpendicular to the needle; *wrap yarn around under the needle and then wrap yarn over crochet hook and pull through the st on the hook*. There is now 1 st on the needle and 1 st on the hook.

3. Rep from * to * until you have the appropriate number of sts on the needle.

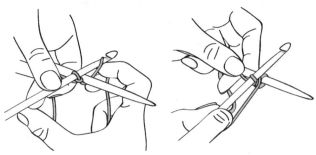

4. When you have cast on the correct number of sts, pull end of yarn through final st on crochet hook and put a knot at end of yarn to mark the end where you will later unravel the chain.

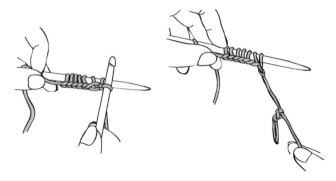

5. Switch to the project yarn and begin knitting.

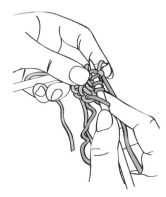

When you need to remove the provisional cast-on, unravel the crochet chain starting at the marked end. Carefully place each of the live stitches on a needle and begin working.

binding off
Elastic Bind-Off
K1, *k1, sl 2 sts to LH needle, k2tog tbl, rep from *to end.

I-cord Bind-Off
CO 3 sts at start of row, *k2, ssk, place all 3 sts back on LH needle and rep from *.

Three-Needle Bind-Off
1. With RS of both pieces together, hold the 2 needles parallel in the left hand with the WS facing you.
2. [Insert the third needle into the first st on the front needle and the first st on the back needle and knit these 2 sts together] twice. Pass the outer st on the RH needle over the st just made to BO 1 st.

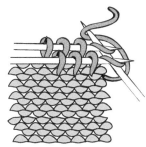

3. *Insert the third needle into the first st on the front needle and the first st on the back needle, knit these 2 sts together, then pass the outer st on the RH needle over the st just made to BO 1 st; rep from * until 1 st remains on RH needle.
4. Cut yarn and pull tail through the last st to secure.

buttonholes
One-Row Buttonhole
NOTE: *All sts are slipped purlwise.*

1. Work to buttonhole position: Sl 1 wyif, move yarn to back, sl 1, pass first slipped st over newly slipped st. [Sl 1, pass the previous st over the newly slipped st] 2 times, then move resulting st back onto LH needle.
2. Turn work; *CO 4 sts using the cable cast-on method.
3. Turn work again; sl 1 from LH to RH needle and pass the last cast-on st over it and continue in pattern to next buttonhole.

decreases
You can work decreases (dec) in a variety of ways; each decrease method creates a different effect. Below I've described the different decreases I used in the book as well as the slant they create. If a decrease isn't described in detail in a pattern, then use the one you think will produce the desired result. For purled

decreases, I have described the slant they create on the RS (or knit side) of the work.

Cdd

Centered double decrease: Sl 2 sts together as though to k2tog, k1, pass 2 slipped sts over.

K2tog

Right-slanting decrease: Knit 2 sts together. (1 st dec'd.)

P2tog

Right-slanting decrease (on RS of work): Purl 2 sts together. (1 st dec'd.)

P2tog tbl

Left-slanting decrease (on RS of work): Purl 2 sts together through their back loops. (1 st dec'd.)

P3tog

Right-slanting decrease (on RS of work): Purl 3 sts together. (2 sts dec'd.)

Ssk

Left-slanting decrease: Slip 2 sts knit-wise, one at a time, then knit those 2 sts together. (1 st dec'd.)

Sssk

Left-slanting decrease: Slip 3 sts knit-wise, one at a time, then knit those 3 sts together. (2 sts dec'd.)

Ssp

Left-slanting decrease (on RS of work): Slip 2 sts knit-wise, one at a time, return sl sts to LH needle, then purl these 2 sts together through back loop. (1 st dec'd.)

increases

As with decreases, you can work increases in a variety of different ways. Increases are often less obvious than decreases and the slant created is more subtle. The increases listed below are not a comprehensive list; feel free to use your preferred increase method to produce the desired result.

Kfb

Bar increase: Knit into the front and back of the same st. This creates a "bar" across the bottom of second st created. This can be used as a decorative feature when repeated. (1 knit st inc'd.)

M1

Make 1 stitch; work either M1R or M1L when m1 is called for in a pattern. Ensure you work the same increase consistently throughout work. (1 knit st inc'd.)

M1L

Left-slanting increase: Insert LH needle from front to back under the horizontal running thread between sts. Knit into back of this st to twist closed. (1 knit st inc'd.)

M1R

Right-slanting increase: Insert LH needle from back to front under the horizontal running thread between sts. Knit into front of this st to twist closed. (1 knit st inc'd.)

M1P

Insert LH needle from front to back under the horizontal running thread between sts. Purl into back of this st to twist closed. (1 purl st inc'd.)

Pfb

Bar increase: Purl into the front and back of the same st. Creates a "bar" across bottom of second st created on the RS (knit) of work. (1 purl st inc'd.)

special techniques

Applied I-cord

1. Using circular needles and with RS facing, pick up sts from right to left along the edge you want to apply I-cord. After all sts are picked up, slide sts to other end of needle to work.

2. Using dpn, CO 3 sts. *K2, ssk using the last st on the dpn and first st on the circular needle. Slide all sts to the other end of dpn, pull snugly and rep from * until all picked up sts have been worked.

Grafting (Kitchener Stitch)

Place an equal number of sts on the front and back needles; break yarn leaving a generous tail. Thread a tapestry needle with the yarn. Hold both needles parallel to each other. It is helpful to lay them on a table in the position they need to be worked in.

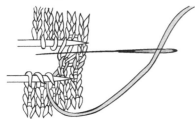

1. Pull needle through first front st as if to purl.

2. Pull needle through first back st as if to knit.

3. Pull needle through first front st as if to knit and slip st off needle. Pull needle through next front st as if to purl, but leave st on needle.

4. Pull needle through first back st as if to purl and slip st off needle. Pull needle through next back st as if to knit, but leave st on needle.

5. Repeat steps 3 and 4 until all sts have been worked.

Take care to pull yarn carefully through worked stitches periodically. Make sure you do not work it too tightly; it should look like a knitted stitch.

Whipstitch

I use whipstitch in this book to join folded hems. Fold the work into the position you want to join it in. For the patterns in this book, the front stitches are still live.

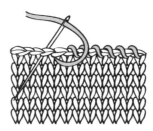

Thread yarn on a tapestry needle with long tail and working from right to left, *pull needle from top to bottom through knitting at back (I always pick a specific row of "loops" to ensure my seam is straight) and then from the back to front of top stitch; rep from * until seam is complete.

Wrap & Turn (w&t)

Wrap & turns (abbreviated as w&t) are used to work short rows. When working a "short row," you wrap the stitch to avoid a gap at the point where you want to turn the work. When you pass the wrap again, you will need to work it with the stitch it wraps in order to avoid seeing the wrap in the finished work.

On a knit row:

1. Work to last st before wrap, sl next st purl-wise to RH needle, pass yarn from back to front, slip st back to LH needle.

2. Turn to work purl row, passing yarn to front of work. When you work the next st, make sure you pull yarn snugly enough so there is no gap. Take care not to pull so tightly that you distort the st.

On a purl row:

1. Work to last st before wrap, sl next st purl-wise to RH needle, pass yarn from front to back, slip st back to LH needle.

2. Turn to work knit row, passing yarn to back of work. When you work the next st, make sure you pull yarn snugly enough so there is no gap. Take care not to pull so tightly that you distort the st.

When you come to a wrapped stitch in subsequent rows:

- **For knit sts:** Lift the wrap onto the RH needle from the front and work it together with the st it wraps.

- **For purl sts:** Lift the wrap with RH needle from the *right side* of the work and place on the LH needle. Work together with the st that it wraps.

knitting abbreviations

ABBREVIATION	MEANING
[ ]	work instructions within brackets as many times as directed
* *	repeat instructions between asterisks as directed
"	inch(es)
alt	alternating (every other)
beg	beginning
BO	bind off (cast off)
cdd	Centered double decrease: Slip 2 stitches together as though to k2tog, k1, pass 2 slipped stitches over.
circ	circular
cm	centimeter(s)
CN	cable needle
CO	cast on
dec	decrease(ing)
dec'd	decreased
dpn(s)	double-pointed needle(s)
est'd	established
g	gram(s)
inc	increase(ing)
inc'd	increased
k	knit
k2tog	knit 2 stitches together
kfb	knit into front and back of stitch
kfpb	knit into front of stitch, purl into back of stitch
k-wise	knitwise
LH	left hand
m	marker or meter
m1	make 1 stitch; use M1L or M1R
M1L	Make 1 stitch (left slant): Insert left-hand needle from front to back under the horizontal running thread between stitches. Knit into back of this stitch to twist closed.
M1R	Make 1 stitch (right slant): Insert left-hand needle from back to front under the horizontal running thread between stitches. Knit into front of this stitch to twist closed.
m1p	Make 1 purl stitch. Insert left-hand needle from front to back under the horizontal running thread between stitches. Purl into back of this stitch to twist closed.
mm	millimeter(s)
oz	ounce(s)
p	purl
p2tog	purl 2 stitches together

ABBREVIATION	MEANING
p2tog tbl	purl 2 stitches together through back loop
p3tog	purl 3 stitches together
patt	pattern
pfb	purl into front and back of stitch
pfkb	purl into front of stitch, knit into back of stitch
pm	place marker
psso	pass slipped stitch over
p-wise	purlwise
rem	remain(ing)
rep	repeat
rev St st	reverse stockinette stitch
RH	right hand
rnd(s)	round(s)
RS	right side
sl 1	slip 1 stitch (purlwise)
sl 1 k-wise	slip 1 stitch knitwise
sl 1 wyif	slip 1 stitch with yarn in front of work
sm	slip marker
ssk	slip 2 stitches, one at a time, as if to knit, then knit those 2 stitches together
sssk	slip 3 stitches, one at a time, as if to knit, then knit those 3 stitches together
ssp	slip 2 stitches knit-wise, one at a time, return slipped stitches to left-hand needle, then purl these 2 stitches together through back loop
st(s)	stitch(es)
St st	stockinette stitch (stocking stitch)
tbl	through back loop
tog	together
w&t	wrap and turn (for short rows)
WS	wrong side
wyib	with yarn in back
wyif	with yarn in front
yd	yard(s)
yo	yarn over

Learn more about the highlighted terms in the "Knitting Techniques" appendix.

KNITTING RESOURCES

I love to have a combination of different knitting books on the bookshelf; they provide inspiration, assistance, and encouragement. I've divided some of my favorite books into different groups because they are all useful in different ways. Hopefully, you'll find something here to fill a gap in your knitting library!

KNITTING BOOKS

Construction and Techniques

A general knitting construction book can give you a good understanding about the basics of garment construction, and every knitter should own at least one finishing book!

- *The Knitter's Bible* (David & Charles, 2004), by Claire Crompton
- *The Knitter's Book of Finishing Techniques* (Martingale & Company, 2002), by Nancie M. Wiseman
- *Knitting from the Top* (Schoolhouse Press, 1996), by Barbara G. Walker
- *Knitting on the Edge* (sixth&spring books, 2004), by Nicky Epstein
- *Knitting Workshop* (Schoolhouse Press, 1981), by Elizabeth Zimmermann
- *Sweater Design in Plain English, 2nd Edition* (St. Martin's Griffin, 2011), by Maggie Righetti and Terri Shaw

Stitch Guides

When working with cable patterns, these stitch guides are some of the most useful I've found. It is, of course, by no means a definitive list. Stitch guides provide guidance when you wish to substitute a pattern stitch or create your own unique garment from scratch.

- *The Harmony Guides 220 Aran Stitches and Patterns: Volume 5* (Anova Books, 1998)
- *A Treasury of Knitting Patterns, volumes 1–4* (Schoolhouse Press, 1998/2000), by Barbara G. Walker

Inspiration

These books don't fall under either of the previous headings, but if you enjoy working with cables then you are sure to find inspiration between their covers.

- *Aran Knitting: New and Expanded Edition* (Dover Publications Inc., 2010), by Alice Starmore
- *Power Cables: The Ultimate Guide to Knitting Inventive Cables* (Interweave Press, 2010), by Lily M. Chin

yarn availability and substitutions

All of the yarns used in this book are produced or dyed in Ireland. They are available for sale online with worldwide shipping; details are listed below. Additionally, I've provided known U.S. suppliers of the Irish yarns used in this book as well as recommendations for yarn substitutions for each of the mills. (The information below was correct at the time of writing.) Please note that yarn names and colors frequently change. To ensure you have the correct yarn or substitution, take care to match the gauge listed in the pattern with the suggested gauge of the yarn you are purchasing. For assistance with yarn choices, Web sites like www.yarndex.com and www.ravelry.com or your local yarn store can provide invaluable help.

irish yarn sources

Cushendale Woollen Mills

www.cushendale.ie

All yarns are available directly from the mill. The retail store also sells yarn in Graig-Na-Managh, County Kilkenny, Ireland.

U.S. Supplier

Black Water Abbey Yarns
P.O. Box 470688
Aurora, CO 80047-0688
720-320-1003
www.abbeyyarns.com

Suppliers of Cushendale Woollen Mills yarn in the United States. "DK Wool" (used in some of this book's patterns) is sold as "2-ply Worsted," and "4-ply/Sportweight" is sold as "2-ply Sportweight" in the United States.

Donegal Yarns

www.donegalyarns.com

NOTE: Previously known as Kilcarra Yarns, some shops and online retailers may still sell the yarn under this label as well as the "Studio Donegal" label.

All yarns are available directly from the mill in 1 or 2kg (2–4.5 lb.) cones.

Knoll Yarns Limited

www.knollyarns.com

International distributor of "Aran Tweed," but sold as "Kilcarra Tweed."

Studio Donegal

www.studiodonegal.ie

At press time, Studio Donegal only sells "Aran Tweed" yarn. They are, however, planning to have "Soft Donegal" yarn also available soon. The retail store is located in Kilcar, County Donegal, Ireland.

Kerry Woollen Mills

www.kerrywoollenmills.ie

All yarns are available directly from the mill. The retail store also sells yarn in Beaufort, Killarney, County Kerry, Ireland.

U.S. Suppliers

Black Water Abbey Yarns
P.O. Box 470688
Aurora, CO 80047-0688
720-320-1003
www.abbeyyarns.com

Suppliers of 2-ply fingering weight wool (*spun by Kerry Woollen Mills*) which can be held double and used as a substitute for Kerry Woollen Mills' "Organic 2-Ply" yarn.

Irish Imports Ltd
1737 Massachusetts Avenue
Cambridge, MA 02138
1-800-356-2511
www.irishimportsltd.com

This company buys Irish-milled yarn, but you may need to contact the shop directly to inquire about the specific yarns they stock.

irish hand dyers

Dublin Dye Company
Etsy store: http://www.etsy.com/shop/dublindyeco

All yarns are available directly from Dublin Dye Company's Etsy store.

This Is Knit (yarn store)
www.thisisknit.ie

Online retailer and retail store in Dublin, Ireland.

Hedgehog Fibres
Etsy store: www.etsy.com/shop/hedgehogfibres
Blog: www.fly-along.blogspot.com

All yarns are available directly from dyer.

This Is Knit (yarn store)
www.thisisknit.ie

Online retailer and retail store in Dublin, Ireland.

Other Irish Hand Dyers (not featured in book)

Gaiety Girl
http://www.etsy.com/shop/gaietygirl
These yarns are also available at www.thisisknit.ie

Laura Hogan
http://www.etsy.com/shop/LHogan

other irish yarn online retailers

These Irish online retailers sell some of the yarns from the three Irish mills discussed in this book. Check with each individual site regarding worldwide shipping availability and costs.

Commodum
www.commodum.ie

The Constant Knitter
www.theconstantknitter.com

Crafter's Basket
www.craftersbasket.com

Spring Wools
www.springwools.com

The Yarn Emporium
http://theyarnemporium.com

The Yarn Room
www.theyarnroom.com

This Is Knit
www.thisisknit.ie

yarn substitutions

Listed below are some yarns that are easy to find in the United States and would make good substitutions for the yarns used in this book.

Cushendale Woollen Mills

Suitable "DK Wool" substitutions:
- *Cascade 220* by Cascade Yarns
- *Peruvian Highland Wool* by Elann
- *Purelife British Sheep Breeds DK* by Rowan

Suitable "4-ply/Sportweight" substitutions:
- *Double Knitting* by Jamieson's
- *Telemark* by Knit Picks

Donegal Yarns

Suitable "Aran Tweed" and "Donegal Soft" substitutions:

NOTE: Both of these yarns have similar gauges; therefore, they can be used interchangeably for all Donegal Yarns patterns.

- *City Tweed HW* by KnitPicks
- *Donegal Luxury Tweed Aran* by Debbie Bliss
- *Donegal Tweed* by Tahki Yarns
- *Irish Tweed* by MaggiKnits
- *Shelter* by Brooklyn Tweed

Kerry Woollen Mills

Suitable "Aran Wool" substitutions:
- *Heather Aran* by Jamieson's
- *Heritage* by Briggs and Little
- *New England Highland* by Harrisville Designs

Suitable "Organic 2-ply" substitutions:
- *Double Knitting* by Jamieson's
- *Nature Spun Sport* by Brown Sheep

index

about the author

Carol Feller is an independent knitwear designer and knitting teacher. Her design approach combines her training as both an artist and a structural engineer, emphasizing seamless construction and clever shaping techniques to create flattering, tailored garments with interesting shapes and textures. Her patterns for men, women, and children are widely published in books and magazines, including Knitting in the Sun (Wiley, 2009), More Knitting in the Sun (Wiley, 2011), Twist Collective, Interweave Knits, Knitty, and Yarn Forward. You can find her self-published patterns and e-books on her website (www.stolenstitches.com) and on Ravelry (www.ravelry.com/designers/carol-feller). Carol blogs on stolenstitches.com and can also be found on Twitter (stolenstitches), Ravelry (littlefellers), and Facebook (carol.feller). She lives in Cork, Ireland, with her husband, four sons, and a large dog.

CPSIA information can be obtained at www.ICGtesting.com
Printed in the USA
LVOW02s1440180214

374216LV00010B/31/P

9 780470 889244